Adolescence
and Religion

Adolescence
and Religion

The Jewish Teenager in American Society

By BERNARD CARL ROSEN

SCHENKMAN PUBLISHING COMPANY, INC.

Cambridge, Massachusetts

"TEMPLE ISRAEL"

For Shirley and Michele

CONTENTS

The Social Context: Reference Groups.
Primary and Secondary Referents. The
Reference Group Concept. The Reli-
gious Self-Estimation and The Reference
Group. Individual Models. Group Mod-
els. Conceptualized Models. The Anchor
Reference Groups. The Intermediate
Reference Group.

The Parent as Significant Other. The
Parent as Religious Referent. The Expectations of Parents. Parental Behavior
and Adolescent Religiosity.

The Formal Youth Groups. The Reli-
gious Influence of Formal Groups. The
Informal Youth Groups. The Informal
Peer Group and Religion. The Peer
Group as Reference Group. Parent-Peer
Group Cross-Pressures.

The Cross Pressure Situation. Some
Characteristics of the Yorktown Jewish
Community: Size. Economic Status and
Place of National Origin. Organizations.
Group Pressures and Ethnic Separate-
ness. Intermarriage Taboo. The Soror-
ity's New Year's Eve Dance. Formal
Community Influences on Adolescent
Religiosity. The Jewish Center. The
Religious School. Type and Length of
Religious Schooling. The Information
Test. The Influence of the School on

Religious Attitudes and Behavior. Informal Community Pressures on the
Adolescent. Community Religious Expectations.

Uniformity and Conformity. Seculariza-
tion and Religion. Equalitarianism and
Religion. A Further Note on Societal
Pressures.

Individual Identification. Group Identification. Categorical Identification. Referential Identification. Group Identity and
Religion. Religion and Recognition of
Ethnic Identity. Religion and Meaning
of Jewish Identity. Ethnic Identity and
Adolescent Religiosity. Group Identification and Adolescent Religiosity. The
Identification Index. Identification and
Group Survival. Identification and Assimilation.

Adolescent Religious Attitudes and Be-
havior: An Overview. Drift and Selectiv-
ity. Discrepancy between Attitudes and
Behavior. Regional Similarities and Dif-
ferences. Positive Orientation Toward
Religion. Group Factors in Adolescent
Religiosity. Location of Significant Re-
ferents. The Family. The Peer Group.
The Ethnic Group and the General
Society. Information and its Uses: A
Concluding Note.

Tables

PREFACE

Possibly no group has been examined, interpreted and admonished for so long a period and with such frequency as the Jews. From biblical times until the present numerous authors, both from within and outside the group, have written seemingly innumerable articles and books in answer to the questions: Who are the Jews? What do they believe? How do they behave and why? I am not so ambitious, or foolhardy, as to attempt to answer all or even any of these questions in an exhaustive way. Rather, I have sought to focus attention on one aspect of Jewish life — religion, or more specifically the religious attitudes and behavior of Jewish adolescents in four cities in the United States.

As an adolescent I was struck by how little adults understood teenagers. As an adult I realize how difficult it is, in fact, for parents to comprehend their progeny and how little hard information is available for their guidance. So, I have devoted a portion of this book to a description of some aspects of the religious convictions and conduct of Jewish adolescents which I hope will be of value to parents, interested laymen and professional workers.

But this volume is meant to be more than a description of what adolescents say and do. It is the "why" of adolescent attitudes and behavior which most excites my interest. Hence, the aim of this book has been to contribute to our understanding of the social psychology of attitude and behavior formation. Its principal focus is on the impact of the group upon the adolescent's religious attitudes and behavior. The Jewish adolescent shares with other teenagers membership in such groups as the family and the peer group, but he is also a member of a minority ethnic group. Much of the discussion which follows will revolve around this fact.

Some aspects of the problem and a portion of the data examined in this book have been reported elsewhere in three articles which I authored. They are: "Multiple Group Membership: A Study of Parent-Peer Group Cross-Pressures," *American Sociological Review,* April, 1955, pp. 155–161; "The Reference Group Approach to the Parental Factor in Attitude and Behavior Formation," *Social Forces,* December, 1955, pp. 137–144; "Minority Group in Transition," in *The Jews: Social Patterns of an American Group,* Marshall Sklare, (Editor), Glencoe: The Free Press, 1958.

This book has been some time in the making, and over the years I have accumulated far more debts than I can possibly acknowledge in this space. I would, however, like to mention a number of people who became directly involved in the conduct of the research. I am indebted to Robin M. Williams for his lucid analysis of American society and for the guidance both he and Edward A. Suchman gave me during the Yorktown phase of the research. The research in Yorktown was conducted while I was associated with the Cornell Studies in Intergroup Relations. I wish to express my appreciation to the Studies' directors Robin M. Williams, Edward A. Suchman and John P. Dean for their support and counsel.

I am indebted to the Bureau of Applied Social Research, Columbia University, and to the Departments of Sociology at Cornell University and the University of Nebraska for making available their data processing facilities. Thanks are due to

Jessie Cohen of Cornell University for her assistance in the statistical analysis of some aspects of the data, and to Peter Rossi, of the University of Chicago, who did the latent structure scaling.

Also I wish to acknowledge the friendly assistance of the many social workers and directors of youth centers, Jewish and non-Jewish, in Pennsylvania, New York and Nebraska who offered their facilities in which to make contact with Jewish adolescents. In particular, I am grateful to Alex Rosen, at the time of this study Director of the Jewish Center in Yorktown (a fictitious name, for obvious reasons) who was exceptionally helpful. I shall always remember the adolescents and adults of Yorktown with great affection; without their friendly cooperation this study could never have been accomplished. I want also to express my appreciation to Harry Gratz for his help in collecting the data in Philadelphia, and to Earl Yaillen who was helpful in the collection of the Nebraska data.

Part of this research was supported by the Anti-Defamation League of B'nai B'rith which twice awarded me a Sigmund Livingston Fellowship. I am grateful to Robin Williams and Leo Srole, formerly Director of the League's Research Branch, who made these fellowships possible.

I wish also to express my appreciation to the National Institute of Mental Health, United States Public Health Service, whose research grant (M-05589) enabled me to stay in Brazil for nineteen months. While the grant did not directly support this research, it did subsidize a leave of absence from the University of Nebraska, freeing me from teaching responsibilities so that I could devote full time to research and writing. I am indebted to the University of Nebraska for granting so long a leave of absence and especially to Alan P. Bates who did so much to make it possible. I am also grateful to Senhor Francisco de Azevedo, Director of the Biblioteca Municipal Mario de Andrade, who provided me with a handsome office while I was in São Paulo.

I was fortunate enough to have my family with me while in Brazil. My wife, Shirley, was a source of encouragement during the book's gestation period and performed a yeoman service by typing the manuscript under very difficult conditions; while my daughter, Michele, merely by being herself gave me the courage to start each new chapter.

                                                    Bernard Carl Rosen

São Paulo
   1964
Lincoln, Nebraska
   1965

Introduction

The American adolescent is the pride and puzzlement of his parents. To many a fond but bewildered parent, the adolescent often appears at odds with himself and discontented. This seems anomalous in a society which glorifies youth, physical vigor and attractiveness, prides itself on being modern and up-to-date and devotes enormous amounts of time and money on its youngsters. By any measure the attention which the American adolescent commands is impressive. Industries gear themselves to satisfy his needs; popular culture panders to and is molded by his tastes; while in the movies, on television and the like he is constantly reminded that youth is the ideal time of life. And yet, notwithstanding the attention he enjoys, the teenager not infrequently appears confused; his behavior at times seems erratic, disorganized, even queer.

In response to the need to understand what lies behind adolescent behavior and to help the parent and society in general cope with this complex phenomenon, there has emerged in recent years a truly impressive mass of empirical research, theoretical analysis and popular diagnosis. At the popular level, the view of adolescence and adolescents tends to be one of alarm. Numerous magazine and newspaper columnists have written innumerable and often excruciating articles on the adolescent's "problems." So prolific and ubiquitous are these analysts that the family supplement of most Sunday newspapers seems hardly complete without at least one article on the difficulties adolescents have with their families, peers or the general society.

The view from academia, while somewhat less problem-oriented, has also been reported in a prolific (some would say prolix) literature. The American adolescent has been viewed developmentally by educators (Bernard, 1957), behavioristically and psychoanalytically by psychologists (Jersild, 1957; Blos, 1962) and in a social context by sociologists (Smith, 1962; Gottlieb and Ramsey, 1964).

With each year we know more about when the adolescent enters cliques (Gordon, 1957), whom he admires among his peers (Coleman, 1961), what affects his performance in school (Rosen, 1956), which occupations he aspires to (Ginzberg, et al., 1961), why he becomes delinquent (Cloward and Ohlin, 1960), and how his personality compares with adolescents from other countries (Rosen, 1964a) — to name just a few areas in which research has been undertaken. But what he thinks about his religion and the degree to which he observes its rules, and why, is possibly one of the least researched areas in contemporary American life.

Part of the reason for this is the general neglect of religion as an area of research in American social science. Thus, in every census of social research in the past fifteen years, studies in the sociology of religion have made up a small fraction of the total. There have been, it is true, several studies of small sects or of professional roles within religious groups (Clark, 1949), but empirical investigations of the religious conduct and convictions of the general membership, particularly adolescents, have been surprisingly few. Surprising not merely because interest in religion appears to have increased since World War II, but also because religion is a particularly appropriate area of research for anyone interested in youth, since it is often in adolescence that the individual first questions the religious tenets taught to him as a child. The confusion and anxiety which uncertainty in this area could engender should be of special interest to anyone interested in adolescents.

When the adolescents are Jews there is an additional element of interest, partly because of the adjustments in religious orientations which Jews have had to make in adapting themselves to the majority culture of American society. And yet not since a study of Franzblau (1934), has much been added to our knowledge about the religiosity of Jewish adolescents. With few exceptions, studies in this area have been highly impressionistic and value-laden. Most of the carefully collected empirical information on the religious attitudes and behavior of Jewish youth, with the conspicuous exception of the Riverton study (Sklare and Vosk, 1957), have been obtained from college students — an older and more select population than the generality of Jewish adolescents (Nathan, 1932; Ross, 1950; Rossman, 1960).

The need for information is clear. Many adults, even those professionally concerned with the religious lives of adolescents, are not adequately informed (some are misinformed) as to the religious convictions and conduct of Jewish youth. Parents who try to get their children to attend religious services, rabbis who struggle to arouse the interest of adolescents in the activities of their synagogue or temple, and social workers who attempt to include religious elements into the programs of Jewish Centers are often frustrated in their efforts by an inadequate understanding of the religious orientation of Jewish teenagers. Religious educators, in particular, often operate with an insufficient awareness of the religious orientation of their teenage students, and with little informed knowledge of the effects of their teaching upon the pupil's attitudes and behavior.

Hence, a portion of this work will be devoted to satisfying the need for simple, factual information. We shall examine such questions as: What are the attitudes of Jewish adolescents toward certain traditional religious beliefs and practices? For example, do they believe in a personal deity? How often do they attend religious services? How do they feel about the food laws?

Description by itself, no matter how useful an inventory of attitudes and behavior may be, is not sufficient, however. We also need to understand the factors which influence the formation of religious attitudes and behavior. Hence, the major part of this volume will be devoted to an examination of some group-related factors which affect the adolescent's religious convictions and conduct. Until relatively recently most quantitatively based studies of attitudes did not go beyond the description level. Others, at best, limited the analysis to an examination of the relationship of one set of attitudes to another set of attitudes or to some single physical or social attribute. Thus, religious attitudes would be related to political attitudes; or religious behavior would be related to sex, or education (Starbuck, 1899; Clark, 1929; Newcomb and Svehla, 1937; Argyle, 1959).

In the past twenty-five years, a number of empirical studies have re-emphasized the importance of understanding the influence of group norms and other group factors in any interpretation of the individual's attitudes and behavior. A generation ago in a classic study Sherif (1935) was able to demonstrate that the individual's judgment is formed with the context of his membership in groups and their norms. Although there have been numerous studies of this type since that time, many areas are as yet un-examined. This study is an attempt to fill a small part of the lacunae that exist in our knowledge of the influence of group membership on religious attitudes and behavior.

The basic concern of this study is to show how the religious attitudes and conduct of Jewish adolescents are related to their membership in certain groups and to their sense of identification with these groups.

Much of the analysis which follows will be devoted to (1) locating the groups that are significant to the adolescent; and (2) determining whether a relationship exists between the adolescent's religiosity, his membership and identification with these groups, and the groups' religiosity, expectations and pressures.

Four groups were singled out for examination; the family, the peer group, the minority group, and the national society. The nature of these groups and the reasons for their inclusion in this study are specified in later chapters. An examination will be made of the pressures they exert upon the adolescent, their expectations as far as religion is concerned, and the relationship of these pressures and expectations to the adolescent's religiosity. We shall also want to know the conditions under which models for self-estimation become "significant others," whether there is a relationship between the adolescent's perception of the expectations of others and his religiosity, and the role of religion in the adolescent's conceptualization of his ethnic identity.

THE PLAN OF PRESENTATION

This volume is divided into six parts. Part I (Chapters 1 and 2) discusses the problem on which the research was focused, describes briefly when, where and how the data were collected, and explains the specific usage of certain key terms. Part II specifies the dependent variable — some religious beliefs and practices of traditional Judaism, the attitude of adolescents toward them and the degree to which they were observed. This is done in two Chapters — one dealing with beliefs, the other with practices.

Part III outlines a major portion of the conceptual framework within which the data are interpreted.

Parts IV and V examine the independent and intervening variables. They analyze some of the group factors which influence the religious convictions and conduct of Jewish adolescents. There are two Chapters in Part IV, one devoted to the family, the other to the peer group. They examine the relationship between the adolescent's religiosity and his membership in these two important primary groups. Part V is composed of three chapters. The first two specify the social contexts created by the ethnic and national groups and the pressures they exert upon the adolescent. A third Chapter analyzes the relationship between religious attitudes, behavior and group identification. Part VI, the concluding Chapter, summarizes the findings of the study.

Chapter Two

Scope and Method

Before intelligent questions about Judaism's beliefs, practices and institutions can be asked, we must first know what they are. This is no easy task. There has never been complete consensus among Jews about the beliefs and practices of their religion. Even in biblical times and during the era of the great academies controversy over religious doctrine and practice was common (Graetz, 1898). The dissolution of the Great Synhedrion in the reign of Emperor Constantius eliminated the one group sufficiently accepted and authoritative to make doctrinal decisions and to keep sectarianism at a minimum. Gradually, differences developed between the practices of Western Jewry and those of Eastern Jewry. Later, Western Jewry divided into two groups — the Spanish or Sephardic, and the German-East European or Ashkenazic.

The process of differentiation and change was accelerated in the 18th and early 19th centuries. In many European countries, notably those lands which felt most directly the force of the

French Revolution, the Jews were granted increased social, civil and economic privileges. They were encouraged to leave the ghetto and take part in the great intellectual revolution that was sweeping Europe free of old ideas and institutions. The events of this period were of such vital social and economic significance for Western Jewry that they have been subsumed under the title "The Emancipation."

The Emancipation had many far reaching consequences for Western Jewry, one of which was the splintering of Western Ashkenazic Jewry into three denominations, — Orthodox, Reformed and, later in the United States, Conservative (Sklare, 1955). These denominations possess viewpoints which fall along a continuum, the ends of which we shall call traditionalistic and non-traditionalistic. Generally speaking, traditionalists include the Orthodox and an indeterminate number of the Conservative congregations. Non-traditionalists, when affiliated at all, are ordinarily members of reform temples, and some conservative groups (Gordis, 1948; Philipson, 1931).

Nothing short of a lengthy essay could provide an adequate description of the many subtle differences between the rituals and beliefs of the three groups — a task beyond the scope of this volume. For our purposes, it is only necessary to keep a few points in mind. First, it is important to remember that there is no general consensus among American Jews as to what constitutes Judaic doctrine (Steinberg, 1945; Glazer, 1957). Since there is no commonly accepted authority to dictate dogma and practice, each congregation and rabbi is free within fairly broad limits to define its own position. Second, the Reform group — the group which first broke with orthodoxy — has deviated the furthest from Judaism as it was practiced before the Emancipation. Third, the Conservative position represents an attempt to operate between orthodoxy and reformism (Sklare, 1955). Whenever necessary we shall make clear how the various denominations stand upon a particular belief or practice.

The focus of this study, however, will not be on denominational differences. Rather, we are interested in determining where adolescents, whatever their denominational affiliation, stand as regards a code of religious beliefs and practices (*traditionalism*) which for centuries commanded the loyalty of Western Jewry. It is this code, as we shall soon see, which adolescents employ, even today, as the ideal standard against which an individual's religiosity is evaluated — whether he be Orthodox, Conservative or Reform.

The Beliefs and Practices

The beliefs and practices included in the study are acceptable to the Orthodox and most Conservative segments of contemporary Jewry. Orthodox beliefs and practices were selected because they provide a traditionally legitimated base against which the behavior and attitudes of the respondents could be examined. We asked about Orthodox beliefs and practices knowing full well that Jewish groups live by different standards in these matters. Our object was to determine how closely modern adolescents conform to a standard which once enjoyed the almost universal support of Western Jewry.

The following six beliefs were abstracted from Maimonides' "Thirteen Articles of Faith" (Albo, 1898):

(1) Belief in a personal God.
(2) Belief that the Torah (the first five books of the Old Testament) is divine revelation.
(3) Belief in reward and punishment after death.
(4) Belief in a Messiah.
(5) Belief that Moses was a historical figure to whom the Decalogue was revealed on Mount Sinai.
(6) Belief that the Jews are a Chosen People.

The five practices about which questions were asked are as follows:

(1) The use of ritually acceptable foods; i.e., *kosher* food.
(2) The use of separate eating and cooking utensils for meat and dairy products.
(3) Synagogue attendance.
(4) Study of Jewish sacred books.
(5) The observance of the Sabbath and other Holy Days.

These beliefs and practices, of course, do not by any means make up the entire Jewish religion. They did, however, help shape the values and symbols, the customs and institutions, and the general ethos of Jewish communities for many centuries. Their influence is still alive today.

What is a Religious Jew: The Adolescent's Perspective

One of the most difficult tasks in the earlier stages of the study was that of defining certain key terms. What do we mean by religion? What constitutes a religiously observant person? As Cohen and Nagel (1934) have noted, religion has sometimes been defined in terms of dogma, sometimes in terms of social organization and ritual, and sometimes in terms of emotional experience. In which of these senses shall we use the terms religion and religiosity? Lacking Humpty Dumpty's mastery over words (he was able to make words mean "just what I choose them to mean — neither more nor less"), we decided to let the adolescents do the defining.

Jewish adolescents in this study exhibited a high degree of consensus as to what religion and religiosity meant. *Almost without exception they defined religion in terms of religious practice.* Thus, when adolescents were asked to explain their answers to the question, "How religious would you say you are — strongly religious, moderately, only slightly, or not at all religious?" all but six respondents justified their self-estimation in terms of their observance (or lack of observance) of some religious practice. One 16 year old boy, who described himself as moderately religious, explained:

"I don't observe every holiday; I work on Saturday, but I keep kosher in the home. I don't eat *tref* (non-kosher) unless I'm really hungry."

A 17 year old girl felt she was only slightly religious because,

"I only go to the synagogue twice a year maybe. I don't keep the holidays — especially Passover. It's ridiculous. They just put a label on it an it's *pessadik* (acceptable for Passover)."

Respondents were then asked, "How would you describe a strongly religious person?" Once again, the answers indicated that they were defining religion in terms of ritual practices, and religiosity in terms of observance of these practices. Jewish adolescents thought of a *strongly* religious person as a thoroughly orthodox individual who observed the vast majority of traditional practices. Most surprising, perhaps, was the fact that Reform as well as Orthodox respondents used traditional norms as their frame of reference. Said a Reform boy,

"A strongly religious person? Well, I'd say he'd be the kind to go to *Shul* (synagogue) everyday, never eats *tref* — *you know, the kind with the white beard and prayer shawl who holds up every single law of the Jewish religion.*"

No doubt this definition of religion is unsatisfying to theologians, and certainly it falls far short of the sophisticated definitions of Williams James (1902) and Gilbert Murray (1935), but its value for this research is great, in the sense that it is more easily measured and remains within the frame of reference employed by the adolescent.

The term traditionalist occurs repeatedly throughout this work. It is used as an approximation of the word orthodox and refers to a tendency to accept orthodox beliefs and to observe orthodox practices. So few respondents were orthodox, *as they themselves defined the term,* that we felt it best to eschew this label and call persons who somewhat approached the orthodox norm traditionalists.

HOW THE STUDY WAS CONDUCTED

An empirical investigation seldom rises above its methodological antecedents. Therefore, in order to provide the reader with information on which he can base his evaluation of the pedigree, so to speak, of this study, a brief description of the samples and techniques of investigation employed are in order.

Samples and Subjects

Five separate samples from four cities were used in the study: two in Philadelphia, one in Yorktown and two in Nebraska. The largest sample, consisting of 513 adolescents, was secured in Philadelphia during the period 1948–50. Unless otherwise noted, it is this sample to which we refer when we speak of the "Philadelphia" sample. During the summer of 1950, a second and smaller sample of 49 adolescents was selected to form what we shall call the "second Philadelphia" sample.

In effect the third sample is not a sample at all but the entire universe of Jewish adolescents attending school in Yorktown, New York, during the years 1950–52. With the help of Yorktown's Jewish Center *every* Jewish adolescent in Yorktown of high school age was located and interviewed — fifty adolescents in all. The fact that the entire Yorktown adolescent population was studied make the data from this community valuable as a check upon the Philadelphia and Nebraska materials.

The last and second largest group, 247 adolescents, was obtained in 1962–63 from subjects living in two Nebraska cities, Omaha and Lincoln. The research in Nebraska was done primarily to enlarge the geographical composition of the sample. Also of interest was the possibility of making comparisons be-

tween the regional samples, although we recognized the difficulties inherent in attempts to explain differences, if any, between
samples chosen at different periods of time.

No attempt was made to obtain a representative sample of
the entire American Jewish adolescent universe. This was not
our goal. Rather, our focus was upon some group factors which
influence the development of religious attitudes and behavior;
hence, we sought only to obtain a sample sufficiently large and
varied to enable us to study the effects of these factors. The
samples, however, have several important characteristics which
bear upon our problem and deserve being mentioned. First,
most of the boys and girls in these samples were secured by visit-
ing Jewish youth groups, predominantly high school fraternities
and sororities, which are extremely popular among adolescents
in the middle class. A Zionist group, several B'nai B'rith youth
clubs and some Jewish Center groups were also included.
Hence, many of the adolescents had made some minimal recognition of their membership in the Jewish community insofar as
they belonged to a youth group whose membership was entirely
Jewish. This fact alone makes it unlikely that the sample is
representative of the entire population of Jewish youth. Second,
adolescents who do not join clubs, Jewish or otherwise, are
probably under-represented in the Philadelphia and Nebraska
samples. It was partly to counteract this bias that a second
Philadelphia sample was selected. These adolescents were
mostly interviewed in the Neighborhood House, a non-sectarian
social service center, or at the Young Men's Hebrew Association
— both in South Philadelphia. All of these adolescents came
to the centers as individuals; none were members of center
clubs or organizations.

Finally, it should be noted that about three-quarters of the
subjects belonged to Orthodox or Conservative congregations.
Since there are no reliable data on Jewish denominational mem-

test was intended for students attending Hebrew Schools. Pre-testing, however, showed it to be too difficult for our respondents, many of whom no longer were attending a religious school. As a result, a considerable revision of the original test was required before it could be administered to our subjects. This test was not given to the Nebraska and Yorktown samples.

The Personal Interview Schedule

Two separate interview schedules were employed to supplement the questionnaire. One schedule was used in personal interviews with forty-nine Philadelphia teenagers. This schedule was essentially designed to provide a check on the data obtained earlier through a questionnaire from a larger sample.

The second schedule was used in Yorktown. In addition to dealing with the areas examined in the Philadelphia and Nebraska questionnaires, the Yorktown schedule sought to locate the significant groups in the adolescent's environment and to determine their impact upon his religious attitudes and behavior. Most of the interviews with these respondents lasted for approximately two hours.

The Interview Situation

It is an oft-heard catch-phrase that one never talks politics or religion with strangers. Centuries of religious wars, persecution, and innumerable personal quarrels have gone into producing this frame of mind. Religion is believed to be so intensely personal an area, so emotionally laden a topic, that direct questioning will only evoke resistance and resentment. How, then, does one get adolescents to talk honestly and frankly on this subject? At first this seemed to be a formidable obstacle. The thing we feared most was that many adolescents would answer our queries stereotypically — telling us what they thought was acceptable, not what they truly believed.

Obtaining frank and open answers to the questionnaire proved to be much less of a problem than had been feared. We sought to impress upon the adolescent the seriousness of the study and the necessity for honest answers during a preliminary "warm up" orientation period. The purpose and technical aspects of the questionnaire were explained and frankness was encouraged by anonymity and an appeal to their sense of fair play. No one was forced to participate, only one person refused. Respondents were warned that dishonest answers would be detected and their entire questionnaire invalidated. The worried faces and furrowed brows, the biting of pencils, and the general air of catharsis, combined with the frequently non-stereotypic aspect of the data, lead us to believe that their answers were honest.

Somewhat to our surprise the most difficult problem associated with the questionnaire arose not from the adolescent's hesitancy about being frank, but from his reluctance to chose one response among several structured alternatives. In order to reduce their resistance to making a decision of this sort, respondents were asked to make a choice first from the alternatives listed and then to write in whatever qualifying or explanatory comments they felt were necessary to make their position clear. This largely removed any resistance to making a choice, although it complicated the task of analyzing their responses. Interestingly enough except for three questions there were never more than two per cent "other answers" i.e., answers which could not be fitted in logically with the ones offered in the questionnaire. In many cases the "other answers" were considerably less than two per cent. The "write in" data became a very valuable source of information which afforded us additional insight into the factors which shaped adolescent attitudes and behavior.

The personal interview situation was much easier to control, partly because the researcher became a familiar figure in the Jewish community during the year in which interviews took place. The same "warm up" orientation was used and anonymity promised, but in addition we were able to watch the respondent carefully — his face and voice — throughout the interview. Whenever we suspected some concealment, questions were re-worded and repeated. Usually, the respondents, adults and adolescents alike, were quite eager to talk with us; no one approached for an interview ever refused. On the whole, we believe, the personal interview situation was so structured as to elicit a high degree of frank and spontaneous response.

Community Analysis

A portion of this book is devoted to an examination of some of the pressures exerted upon the adolescents by ethnic and national groups. The small Jewish community in Yorktown, New York, about which more will be said later, provided an excellent illustration of the manner in which these pressures are applied, their effectiveness and the areas in which they conflict or converge.

Yorktown is an industrial city in Southwestern New York State. Its population at the time of this study was approximately 60 thousand persons. Through frequent visits over a period of a year, the writer gathered a considerable amount of data about Yorktown's Jewish community, its ethos, organization, and socio-economic structure. During this year strategic informants (the rabbis, Center director, business leaders, social leaders, etc.) were interviewed and the teenagers were observed in their clubs, at informal parties, and on the playing fields. In this way a picture could be formed of the manner in which the community's formal and informal groups were structured and the way in which they exerted control over the adolescent.

For the most part everyone was friendly and eager to help. This was especially true of the girls, who in their enthusiasm elected the writer a honorary member of their sorority — the first male ever to be so honored.

Where the Adolescent Stands: Traditional Beliefs

Through the centuries religion permeated Jewish life. Religion gave the Jew a sense of belonging to a group and a set of values by which he could live. Religious *beliefs* legitimated group separateness, gave the Jew a mission, a goal, the prospects of reward for a life well lived. Religious *practices* prescribed a "daily round of ritual" which provided a sense of continuity with past generations and a feeling of solidarity with the present Jewish community. In short, religion was a unifying, group preserving force (Abrahams, 1896; Wirth, 1928).

It is well known that the Jews and their religion have undergone many changes in the past century and a half. But the kind and extent of change, particularly in regard to the religious attitudes and behavior of young people, is imperfectly understood. For example, how do Jewish adolescents feel about religion, particularly as regards certain traditional religious beliefs and

19

practices? Which practices do they observe? What beliefs do they reject? Why? Answers to these questions could best be found, we thought, by asking the adolescents themselves. The following two chapters chronicle their answers.

In effect, this and the following chapter represent a specification of the dependent variable — some aspects of the adolescent's religious attitudes and behavior. Each belief and practice will be described, denominational differences examined and the adolescent's attitudes toward them presented. In the main, an interpretation of the findings and an examination of the social factors which lie behind them will be delayed until later chapters.

We begin by examining adolescent opinions concerning six important religious beliefs, but first we wish to comment on the method of presentation. Since five independent samples were employed in this study, there are five separate distributions of responses to each question. Each response distribution could be examined separately. We believe, however, that the presentation of the data in this fashion would be awkward, even confusing. Hence, we have chosen to treat the five samples as one whenever the response distributions of the five samples are similar. When the distribution of responses are significantly different from one another, as determined by a statistical technique, the data for each sample distribution will be presented separately.

THE GOD IDEA

Twice a day in synagogues throughout the land a prayer is recited in praise of one God, the creator of Man and the Universe. The concept of one God, theologians maintain, is central to Judaism, a part of its very reason for being (Finkelstein, 1945; Steinberg, 1947).

Besides oneness, God has other attributes: He is incorporeal, omnipotent and omniscient. He is also intensely *personal*. The Jewish image of God is not that of an abstract being ruling the cosmos indifferent of man, but of a deity who takes an active interest in Humanity — collectively and individually. The Old Testament makes numerous references to God's interest in mankind. He is continually concerned with the affairs of man. He speaks to human beings, berates and tests them, and makes demands of them. *He listens to their prayers.*

Judaism has always stressed the accessibility of God to man through prayer. God's grace cannot be bought with lip service, the rabbis have long told their congregations, but through prayer man opens his heart to God and in so doing achieves a closer communion with the Deity.

For centuries Jewish religious leaders resisted any attempt to impersonalize the Deity. This was one of the sins for which Spinoza was excommunicated. But with the Emancipation new forces arose. For the first time, Jews were exposed to the full impact of the secularistic wave that challenged many religious doctrines in Western Europe. The Rationalism and Skepticism which had earlier affected the thinking of non-Jews began to influence the Jews as well (Raisin, 1913). Jews, theologians and laymen alike, began to re-examine the tenets of their religion. Although this process is still continuing, the concept of God has changed little. Today, as in the past, rabbis of all denominations explicitly affirm the personal nature of God.

It is far less certain, however, that young people in their congregations feel the same way. Nor is it clear to what extent modern skepticism has affected the adolescent's belief in God. Do Jewish adolescents accept the traditional viewpoint? Or do they believe in an impersonal God? How many in fact believe in a deity at all? The question was put in this way: "Some people say there is a personal God who can be touched by prayer. Others say God is impersonal and cannot be influenced by prayer. What do you think?"

We found that 68 per cent of the adolescents believed in a personal God; 23 per cent believed God to be impersonal; only five per cent replied that they did not believe in God. The remaining four per cent were "don't knows" and "no answers."

Adolescents who believed in a personal God often associated this concept with some private need. As one Philadelphia teenager put it, "When you believe in God, He'll take care of you and look over you. I feel like talking to Him when I want certain things done." A sixteen-year-old Yorktown girl said, "Sometimes when I'm in trouble or want something badly I believe in a personal God." Occasionally respondents would mention some particular request which had been answered.

Some adolescents were skeptical about the efficacy of prayer. As one 17-year-old boy remarked;

> "It's all in the mind, see. If things happen after prayer, it's a miracle!"

A more sophisticated respondent referred to the cathartic effect of prayer,

> "It's not so much that God can be influenced but what reaction you feel when praying. I feel that at times it helps rid us of troubles and helps us make decisions."

During the interviews we observed confusion and hesitation among many respondents as they responded to this question. A 14-year-old girl confessed,

> "I'm not sure whether or not there's a God. I'm very mixed up." And then as an afterthought, "I don't exactly believe in Him."

Remarks such as "I'm not sure," or "I'm confused on the subject" were not uncommon. One girl wrote, "I need more education on this subject" on her questionnaire.

Despite their confusion about the nature of God, very few teenagers said they were atheists. One 16-year-old girl wrote,

"Sometimes I believe that God is impersonal and sometimes that He is not, but there definitely is a God. It is important to believe in something or there is no sense in living."

THE TORAH

Judaism's sacred book is the Torah — also known as the Pentateuch — which contains the first five books of the Old Testament. Regarded as the most cherished possession of the Jewish people and its strongest symbol of historical continuity and unity, the Torah holds a central position in the synagogue or temple, for it is the presence of the Torah which makes the house of worship different from other places of assembly.

The Torah is a narrative of events from the creation of the world to the death of Moses. But to the Orthodox Jew it is infinitely more than a historical narrative. For him the Torah is the fount of Jewish values, beliefs and practices. In it are set forth the concept of a universal God and an ethical code by which the Jew may live. It prescribes rituals, holy days, and forms of worship; sanctions religious and domestic institutions; and creates a code of religious, civil and criminal law (Glover, 1900).

Although the three Jewish denominations hold the Torah in high esteem, basic disagreement exists as to whether it is a divinely revealed document (Steinberg, 1947). The traditionalists believe the Torah to be a God-revealed book whose content is unequivocally true. To the Orthodox Jew the Torah is the repository of infinite wisdom; all truly worthwhile knowledge can be found there, he believes, if the reader will only apply himself with diligence and intelligence. He accepts without question the narrative, beliefs, and practices as they are set forth in the Torah. He would not, for example, question the biblical account of the world's creation.

A result of this attitude is that traditional Judaism is not susceptible to sudden and rapid change. Changes can and have occurred, for the scripture is subject to interpretation and reinterpretation, but change must be slow and distinctly limited.

The non-traditionalist regards the Torah not as divine revelation, but as the work of many human authors and a product of a long evolutionary process. He cannot accept the Torah as a factual account of the past. Furthermore, he considers the Torah subject to revision as time and necessity requires — just like other works of man.

These antithetical orientations toward the Torah which exist among Jews today stem basically from an acceptance or rejection of the belief that the Torah is a product of divine revelation. What position do adolescents take on this issue? We sought an answer to this question by asking, "Do you think the Torah was written by God, partly by man and God, or entirely by wise men, so that the Jews could have a system of laws?"

Among the teenagers in our samples the traditionalist viewpoint is in the minority. Only 24 per cent saw the hand of God, either totally or in part, in the writing of the Torah. Over half (52 per cent) said the Torah is the work of man alone; 24 per cent replied they did not know what to think.

Although they tend to view the Torah as more a product of human invention than divine revelation, it remains a powerful symbol in the minds of Jewish adolescents, even though for many of them it is a book more revered than read. For example, almost half of the Jewish adolescents in the second Philadelphia sample said that they "were not familiar with the contents of the Torah."

THE CHOSEN PEOPLE IDEA

Every ethnic group believes it is in some significant way different from other groups. Some groups lay claim to a special

purity of racial stock, others to superior culture, still others
to superior vigor. Traditional Jews believe their group to be
the recipient of divine revelations, chosen by God to carry His
message to the nations of the world.

Lest they become puffed with pride, the rabbis have often
reminded the Jews that they are not a superior people, nor do
they have special privileges. Quite the contrary, says the
theologian, election entails special burdens and obligations.
Inasmuch as the Jew knows the Law, he is expected to obey it
explicitly. People ignorant of the Law may transgress, but the
Jew must keep the commandments of the Lord, thus providing
an example to other peoples (Finkelstein, 1945). Traditionalist Jews assumed this role as their badge and mission. Often,
despite the admonishments of their leaders, traditionalists reveal
a sense of being better than, as well as different from, other
people.

In the past the Jew did not mind being different (Philipson,
1894). He was expected to be different in a world where groups
and classes displayed very marked cultural dissimilarities. Indeed, dissimilarities were encouraged as a means of distinguishing one group from another (Baron, 1942). However, the
growth of nationalism and egalitarianism in the 18th and 19th
centuries made it increasingly awkward for the Jews to continue
considering themselves a chosen people. To be chosen may
connote being better, and it is uncomfortable for a group to
consider itself superior in a society where everyone is supposed
to be equal in the eyes of the Law — and of God — and where
cultural uniformity is becoming a national virtue.

Whatever the reason, some non-traditionalists reject the idea
outright; others argue that only so long as the Jews dedicate
themselves to God's law are they chosen, and that other people
who "choose God" are also chosen. The traditionalists, however, remain unchanged in their belief that they are a chosen
people with a unique mission.

Some inkling of where young people stand on this issue can be seen in their responses to the question, "Do you think the Jews are a chosen people?"

Only 29 per cent of the Philadelphia sample believed the Jews to be a chosen people, a slightly larger number (38 per cent) rejected the idea, a large number (28 per cent) just did not know what to think, while five per cent left the question unanswered. When this question was asked of the Yorktown group, 22 per cent accepted the belief, 56 per cent rejected it, 22 per cent answered "don't know" or gave no answer. The Nebraska teenager was somewhat more traditionalistic in this area: 36 per cent felt the Jews are a chosen people, 30 per cent did not, and 34 per cent answered "don't know."

The relatively large percentage of "don't know" answers in the Nebraska group may have resulted from a considerable number of respondents' unfamiliarity with the "chosen people" idea. In the personal interviews in Philadelphia we found that 31 per cent of the sample said they had never heard of the "chosen people" concept. Or it may be, as we shall see in a later chapter that the "don't knows" reflect the ambivalence which this particularistic notion produces in an equalitarian society. The anxiety which this idea creates may have been cloaked in an unwillingness to either accept or reject an ancient, albeit ethnocentric, belief.

THE WORLD TO COME

According to traditional Jewish belief, man was created in the image of God and endowed with an immortal soul. Concepts of immortality in Judaism have ranged from the highly abstract to the very concrete and mundane. More so than most other Jewish ideas, the idea of immortality has enjoyed numerous different interpretations (Finkelstein, 1945).

The concepts of Heaven and Hell, and the notion of punishment or reward after death have long been a part of popular Jewish religion. However, many rabbis frown on this idea, arguing that goodness should be its own reward and that no payment is necessary for the good one does in life. They point to the extremely vague references to an afterlife in the Torah — a situation which has generated much learned controversy for many centuries. Nonetheless, despite the disagreement among theologians, the concepts of Heaven and Hell were quite real to traditionalistic Jews in the very recent past and even today.

As with other beliefs, the non-traditionalist takes a position different from that of the traditionalist. Some non-traditionalists do not consider the concepts of Heaven and Hell to be a legitimate part of Judaism. Others reject the idea of a spatial Heaven and Hell and speak of the immortality of man's spirit which outlives the material body in which it is temporarily confined (Steinberg, 1947).

Where do the young people stand? In adolescence, when life stretches ahead invitingly and death seems remote, do young people ever think of life after death? We asked the Philadelphians in personal interviews, "Have you ever thought of life after death?"

Almost three out of four adolescents replied that they had; some of them indicated that they had thought about it a good deal. One boy told us, "I think about it a lot before I go to sleep." The self-conscious smile that this question brought to the lips of many respondents indicated that immortality is a notion which interests many a supposedly unthinking adolescent. The youngsters were then asked whether they accepted the idea of Heaven and Hell. Almost half (47 per cent) of the respondents replied that they did, 32 per cent rejected the idea, and 21 per cent gave "don't know" answers.

Thus, notwithstanding the shaky theological grounds on which it stands, and the long history of ambiguous and equivocable support which it has received from religious leaders, the concept of reward and punishment after death still seems to have considerable attraction for a sizable proportion of contemporary Jewish youth.

THE MESSIAH

According to Jewish tradition a Messiah will someday cleanse the world of evil and establish a peaceful world community based upon justice and brotherly love. The Messiah, it is believed, will be a human being, a direct descendant of King David chosen by God. The Orthodox Jew confidently awaits the arrival of this Messiah.

It has not always been easy to remain confident, however. There have been numerous claimants to the title of Messiah, some of whom enjoyed great popularity. Through some charismatic quality they succeeded in kindling and capturing the imagination of the people (Baron, 1952). Even the cautious Jewish bourgeoisie were taken in. In time, however, all claimants were rejected, but not before many hopes were dashed, lives changed and fortunes lost. The Messiah idea nonetheless remains a hope to which the Traditionalist holds fast, despite many disappointments.

The non-traditionalist has modified the concept considerably. Rejecting the idea of a personal Messiah, he speaks of a Messianic Age, which will be brought about, not by the work of one man, but through the combined efforts of many men (Steinberg, 1947).

Where do the young people stand on this matter? Which viewpoint commands the strongest support? Somewhat less than a quarter (24 per cent) of the Philadelphia sample said they believed in the Messiah idea, an equal number rejected it, 32 per cent said they were unfamiliar with the idea, and 20 per cent answered "don't know" or left the question unanswered. In Yorktown 28 per cent of the adolescents said they believed in the Messiah idea, 56 per cent rejected it, 16 per cent "don't knows" or "no answers." Again the responses of the Nebraska teenagers were somewhat more traditionalistic: 38 per cent believed that "the Messiah will someday help the Jews," 34 per cent did not, 10 per cent gave a "don't know" answer, 18 per cent left the question unanswered. The Yorktown and Nebraska samples appeared somewhat more informed on this belief: only 18 per cent in each sample claimed to be unfamiliar with the concept.

Since all but a small portion of the respondents have received some Jewish education, it is apparent that the concept has never been stressed in religious schools, perhaps not even taught. It also appears probable that some adolescents who said they understood the concept had only a vague notion of it. Some adolescents equated the Messiah with Jesus, indicating that their source of information may very likely be Christian and not Jewish.

The Messiah idea does not appear to be an attractive idea to a great many adolescents, possibly because large sections of Conservative and Reform Jewry minimize or even reject this particular belief. Moreover, the secure and prosperous position of American Jewry is probably not conducive to an acceptance of the concept of a Messianic savior. Whatever the reasons, never once in our many conversations with Jewish adolescents did the Messiah concept arise as one of the religious beliefs which excited interest or concern.

MOSES

Among his thirteen articles of faith, Maimonides included the belief that Moses was a historical personage and prophet to whom the Decalogue had been given on Mount Sinai. Until recent times this belief was one of the least controversial among Maimonides' articles. But modern critical scholarship has caused some people to question the accuracy of the biblical account of Moses and the Exodus.

Critics point out that historians and archaeologists have not uncovered unequivocable empirical evidence of the Prophet's existence and exploits in Egypt, other than that contained in the Bible (Baron, 1952). Indeed historians are not agreed as to whether the Jews ever actually were in Egypt. No evidence of their expulsion, or even their presence in Egypt can be found in records extant. Hence, it is not surprising that some historians consider Moses a legendary folk hero, at least until factual evidence is found. Other scholars, as Orlinsky (1954) and Elder (1960) have noted, are impressed by archeological evidence which repeatedly supports historical references in the Old Testament and tend to accept the biblical account of the exodus as being substantially correct.

Traditionalists are not troubled by the lack of empirical evidence; they accept without question the narrative found in the Bible. To the traditionalist, Moses was indubitably a historical personage, a leader of his people and the receiver of the Decalogue. As such he holds the highest place in the roster of Jewish prophets.

The non-traditionalists viewpoint is in line with certain schools of critical scholarship. Some non-traditionalists consider Moses to be a mythical character; they regard the story of his receiving the Ten Commandments as merely a didactic device used by a people to explain their history. Others, less radical, speak of the prophet as an early tribal leader whose impact on the Jews was so great that they perpetuated his memory in vastly exaggerated myths and legends.

When this controversy was put to the adolescents in Nebraska and Philadelphia, a little more than half (53 per cent) sided with the traditionalists; 24 per cent believed that Moses was a true historical figure, but rejected the idea that he had received the Ten Commandments from God; only 6 per cent thought that Moses was merely a legendary figure; 17 per cent answered that they didn't know. This question was not asked of Yorktown adolescents.

Probably everyone interested in religion, theologians and laymen alike, would agree that the beliefs we have just examined make up a significant part of Judaism. It is no reflection on their importance to suggest that the average Jew is much less concerned with the beliefs of his religion than its practices, for it is usually in the area of practice and custom that the individual makes his earliest, most frequent, and often most meaningful contact with his religion. We turn now to an examination of some traditional Jewish religious practices, the attitudes of adolescents toward them, and the degree to which they are observed.

Where the Adolescent Stands: Traditional Practices

Religious practices influence almost every aspect of traditional Jewish life. From the moment he arises in the morning, the Orthodox Jew enters into a regimen of religiously-oriented practices which does not cease until he closes his eyes in sleep at the end of the day. The ablutions he makes, the foods he eats, the clothes he wears are all in some way affected by religious custom and practice. Most of these practices are prescribed by ritual law, some are derived from custom or folklore (Glover, 1900; Rosenau, 1903).

This study cannot examine every ritually prescribed practice in traditional Judaism (there are 613 of them!). Rather, we propose to examine a few of the more controversial, not necessarily the most important, so that the position of Jewish adolescents on the current dispute that keeps American Jewry divided into three denominations may be determined.

"TEMPLE ISRAEL"

The Orthodox position which went unchallenged for centuries has been criticized, both from within and outside of the group. Some critics argue that many practices which were functional in the past are meaningless and unreasonably restrictive in a modern society. Others, equally vehement, regard most traditional practices as an important part of their religious heritage. They will not abandon them.

Let us turn to an examination of some practices which have long held an important place in the religious orientation of many Jews. In the process we will be noting the areas in which there are disagreements and spelling out the position adolescents take toward them.

THE DIETARY CODE

Three times a day, perhaps more often, the traditional Jew must bear in mind that certain foods are "clean" and permissible, others "unclean" and forbidden. Only certain meats, fish, or fowl are ritually clean; others are expressly forbidden. The sacred and profane foods are listed in the Old Testament for all to read, first in Leviticus, Chapter 11; and again in Deuteronomy, Chapter 14.

In addition to proscribing certain foods, the Bible warns the Jew against "seething a kid in its mother's milk." This has been interpreted to mean that meat and milk products may not be eaten together, and that separate sets of dishes and utensils must be used — one set for meat, the other for dairy foods.

When the Jew lived in semi-autonomous communities, it was far easier to observe the dietary code than it is today. Contact with non-Jews was largely limited to business activities which frequently could be carried on within the physical confines of the Jewish community. Social intercourse with the Gentile was quite limited and, of course, social eating was impossible. When the Jew traveled food could be obtained from a Jewish family or possibly at a tavern maintained by a co-religionist. We do not mean to imply that it was always easy for the Jew to observe the dietary code. It often caused him great inconvenience and even embarrassment. The Romans, for example, accused the Jews of being anti-social because they never joined in pagan feasts (Radin, 1915). We want merely to stress that he was less tempted to the outside world for he had less need for it and less access to it (Philipson, 1894).

The Emancipation changed the attitude of many Jews toward the dietary code, as it did so many other aspects of his attitude toward religion. It became psychologically as well as physically more difficult to observe the food laws. Jews mingled more freely with the non-Jews, both socially and commercially. New social obligations and temptations abounded, where few had existed before. New social pressures, ideas and values bombarded the Jew from every side. Inevitably the cry went up for change.

Reform Judaism answered this cry by completely discarding the dietary practices. Conservative Jews introduced some modifications, as for example, the notion that it is permissible to eat in restaurants where utensils are not ritually clean if the food is in other respects acceptable. Orthodox Jews are forbidden even this. Theoretically they sanction no change, although they are aware of the grumbling about their rigidity, particularly from their children.

Many Jewish adolescents were quite concerned and articulate about the dietary code. Invariably it was the first topic raised in discussions with them. Some teenagers appeared bothered, worried, even resentful about the food practices and their relations to them. To obtain some understanding of how they felt about the traditional dietary code we began by asking, "Do you eat non-*kosher* food?"

Only four per cent of the adolescents said they never ate non-kosher food, 28 per cent said they ate non-kosher food "some-

times," 68 per cent said "often." When asked if they intended
to use *kosher* meat in their homes after marriage, 24 per cent
replied "yes," 32 per cent "no," while 44 per cent answered
"don't know."

That the dietary laws are frequently a source of inconvenience
and irritation to adolescents is evident in their attitudes toward
change. Yorktown teenagers were asked this question, "It has
been suggested that some of the things in the Jewish religion be
changed; others have said they should not be changed. With
whom do you most agree?"

Two-thirds of the adolescents favored change. When asked,
"What changes do you have in mind?", 55 per cent mentioned
the dietary laws. The following question along similar lines was
put to teenagers in Nebraska and Philadelphia: "Some people
say the Jewish food laws should be changed to suit the changing
ways of the people; others say the laws should not be changed.
How do you feel?" Their responses revealed that many adolescents wanted the food laws changed, but that this sentiment was
stronger in Philadelphia than Nebraska: 68 per cent of the
Philadelphia sample favored change as compared with 51 per
cent of the Nebraska group.

What is perhaps most startling about these data is not that
many teenagers wished to change the food laws, but that so
many were opposed to change, despite the fact that they were
themselves non-observant. The reasons for this apparent para-
dox will be examined in a later chapter when we consider the
role of religion in the adolescent's conception of his identity and
his identification with the minority group.

THE HOLY DAYS

Like other religions Judaism has its share of holy days. The
most frequent is the Sabbath, celebrated every seventh day beginning on Friday at sunset. Some other major holy days are

Yom Kippur (Day of Atonement), *Pesach* (Passover), *Sha-buoth* (Pentecost) and *Rosh Ha-Shanah* (The Jewish New Year).

Most of the holy days are occasions for feasting and rejoicing, some are set aside for solemn contemplations, but on all Jewish tradition forbids work, including household tasks. The Orthodox definition of work is all-inclusive. In addition to work associated with gainful employment, many other activities are prohibited. Fires must not be lit, for to light a fire involves some work, hence, unless warmed by fires lit the previous day, food is eaten cold on the Sabbath; travel is also work, so the family stays at or near home; physical games are also forbidden.

The Sabbath, however, need not be repressive or joyless. Quite the contrary, the Jewish Sabbath is meant to be both festive and relaxing. The "blue" Sabbath is not a Jewish experience or concept. There is nothing in the Jewish ideal of Sabbath to suggest that the day must be spent in joyless idleness. Rather, rabbis say, the injunctions against work are meant to insure that people will take time off from everyday duties to rest their bodies and minds. The sumptuous meal that ushers in the Sabbath eve satisfies the body; and the Talmud urges the Jew to enrich his mind by devoting part of the Sabbath to studying the Torah (Finkelstein, 1945).

Nonetheless, even in ancient and Medieval times the Jew found some Sabbath day rules harassing, particularly the ban against traveling which, if strictly interpreted, would have kept the Jew restricted to a small area around his house. Institutionalized evasions of the law, such as the practice of enclosing a large area with a clothes line, thus creating the illusion that the community was one large household, softened somewhat the restrictions on movement, but usually Sabbath regulations were strongly enforced. Undoubtedly, there were some who tried to circumvent the rigid discipline of the community, probably with little success. The faithful observance of holy days was not merely a matter of personal preference; the community could and did exert pressure when necessary to see that the Law was observed (Baron, 1942). As recently as two generations ago, members of Yorktown's synagogue were fined twenty-five cents for violating Sabbath regulations, especially for non-attendance at religious services.

Modern society has so altered the nature of the Jewish community that it could not, even if it so desired, enforce strict observance of the Law. For one thing, the community no longer has the legal power to enforce Jewish law. Moreover traditional observance of the Sabbath involves economic sacrifices for the observant Jew. The religious prohibition of work on the Sabbath means that the Jewish merchant must, if he is orthodox, close his store on one of the busiest shopping days of the week — Saturday. In a highly competitive economy this can be a serious handicap.

As long as the Jew felt strongly about orthodoxy he was willing to endure painful economic privations. A generation or so ago the Jewish merchants of South Philadelphia, which was then the focal point of Philadelphia Jewry, were almost unanimous in observing the Sabbath. A stranger wandering on a Saturday afternoon on South or Marshall Streets would have found most of the stores tightly closed. Today much has changed. Jewish merchants who close their stores on the Sabbath are the exception and no longer the rule. Even on the most solemn holy days many Jews work, either as entrepreneurs or employees.

Overt behavior would seem to indicate that there has been, at least among adults, a considerable change in attitude towards the observance of the holy days. In order to learn where young people stand in this matter we asked the following question: "Some people say that Jews should not work on the Sabbath or Jewish holy days. Other people say that a man has to make a living and has a right to work when he pleases. Which do you most agree with?"

Adolescents in Philadelphia and Nebraska were somewhat evenly divided on this issue: 43 per cent felt that Jews should not work on holy days while 52 per cent felt that a "man has a right to work when he pleases," five per cent either did not know or left the question unanswered. The wording of this question was made sharp intentionally so as to involve the respondent in the problem, although possibly the strong wording of the non-traditional alternative influenced some of the waverers. Although this question was not asked of Yorktown adolescents, a somewhat similar question, "How do you feel about Jews working on the Sabbath?", revealed that 90 per cent did not oppose working on the Sabbath.

An interesting facet of this problem was uncovered through personal interviews and an examination of comments which some respondents wrote upon their questionnaires. It was found that most Jewish adolescents have adopted the conventional classification of the holy days into two categories — the "high" holy days, and the "lesser" holy days. The "high" holy days are *Rosh Ha-Shanah* and *Yom Kippur;* the other sacred days fall in the "lesser" holy days category. A large number of respondents who oppose working on the holy days were in fact thinking only of the "high" holy days. Their opposition to work did not include the Sabbath or the "lesser" holy days. No doubt some holy days have more prestige and are of greater solemnity than others, but the traditionalist injunction against work does not recognize this categorization; it applies to all holy days.

Probably social and economic pressures are at least partly responsible for this categorization. If work is prohibited only on the "high" holy days the economic and social difficulties associated with holy day observance are reduced. There is some evidence that the adolescents' attitudes toward work on the holy days are influenced by the nature of their parents' occupation. When parental occupation was cross tabulated with the adolescents' attitudes, home environment held constant, it was found that the children of parents who would be hurt most by observing the Sabbath and the holy days, that is, merchants and self-employed salesmen to whom Saturday is an important business day, were *least likely* to oppose working on these days. It is also noteworthy that the reasons adolescents gave for not observing the holy days were almost always economic. A typical comment was made by a 14-year-old boy who observed, "My father has to work on holy days in order to earn money; you can't live entirely on religion."

THE ROLE OF RELIGIOUS STUDY

The Jew is sometimes pictured as a disputative intellectual, continually poring over books or engaging in tedious arguments. Like most stereotypes this picture contains a kernel of truth. The Jews traditionally have valued learning and honored their scholars. The scholar was a privileged person in the Jewish community of the past. The prestige he enjoyed was derived in part from the emphasis placed upon the study of religious law and commentary (Finkelstein, 1945).

Learning is still prized by the Jews, as the numerous stories, many no doubt apochryphal, of Jewish parents who have endured privation in order to educate their sons, testify. But if the emphasis on education has not changed, its nature and goals have. Education for the modern Jew is far more likely to be secular than religious. Today, Jewish adolescents with a scholarly bent turn their energies far more often to Euclid and Newton than to Rashi or Maimonides. In numerous secular public schools and colleges, Jews are educated in the Western tradition with its emphasis upon the humanities and sciences. Religion for the most part is relegated to the curriculum of the Sunday School and Hebrew School. As we shall see in a later chapter, few adolescents receive systematic religious education at home, and our information showed there is some question as to how much is learned in religious schools.

Granted that religious learning was once held in high esteem among Jews, what does it mean to the Jewish adolescent today? How does he feel about the study of Judaism's sacred books? We sought an answer to these questions; first, by asking the teenager whether he agreed or disagreed with this statement: "A Jew can not consider himself educated unless he knows the Talmud and Torah thoroughly". It seems fair to say that until very recently, most East European Jews would have agreed with this statement. To *shtetl* Jews religious education *was* education. The learned men of their community were the Talmudic and Torah scholars. Western secular literature was held in so low esteem that Peretz, the celebrated Yiddish novelist, as a boy had to read Dickens on the sly for fear of being punished (Samuel, 1948). Apparently many Jewish adolescents no longer feel this way. Only 14 per cent of the respondents agreed with the above statement, while 86 per cent disagreed.

It appeared that religion played a very small part in the adolescent's image of the educated Jew. Interviews revealed that the word "education" has a purely secular meaning for the teenager. Religious education appeared to be a concept entirely separated from the more general term "education." As the teenager saw it, one can be "educated" without having more than a superficial grasp of one's religion. But conversely, a person learned only in religious matters would not be classified as educated.

If the young people in this study thought of education largely in terms of secular content, does this mean that they saw no point in studying the Talmud and Torah? We tried to find out by asking this question: "Some people say every Jew should spend part of his time studying the Talmud, others say that this is unnecessary and not worth the time and effort since most of its content is out-of-date. With whom would you most agree?"

In response to this question, 51 per cent of the Philadelphia adolescents felt that the Talmud should be studied, 38 per cent did not believe it was necessary, 11 per cent were uncertain how to respond to this question. However, about a third of the youngsters qualified their negative answers by writing that while they felt it was not necessary to study the Talmud, they did not believe its content was out-of-date. Nebraska teenagers gave an even more traditional response to this item: 69 per cent believed the Talmud should be studied, 26 per cent did not, five per cent left the question unanswered. This presents us with a rather anomalous picture of a considerable number of adolescents who value the traditional literature, but who do not wish to study it. A similar situation, as we have already noted, exists in connection with the Torah.

HOUSE OF WORSHIP

The synagogue or temple was, and in some places still is, the focal point of the Jewish community. In the past almost every sphere of Jewish life, secular as well as religious, was in some measure related to the synagogue (Wirth, 1928). The synagogue was the "house of assembly". It was in the synagogue that the Jews met to carry on the activities vital to the community. Public pronouncements of community-wide importance were ordinarily made in the synagogue. The officers of the synagogue had positions of administrative and juridical importance to the community. (Abrahams, 1896). The synagogue was also the "house of study." The school and synagogue were — and still are — closely associated. Rabbis were frequently teachers of the young as well as religious leaders of the adult. But most important of all, the synagogue was the "house of prayer." For it was religion and the communal participation in prayer that gave the synagogue its distinctive character.

Like many other forces in Jewish life, the synagogue in the United States has changed in several significant ways. Some changes reflect geographical factors: Jews are more dispersed than they were in earlier times. Jewish communities in small towns find it difficult to support a synagogue or temple. Other changes reflect the fact that many functions which were once performed by the synagogue or temple have been taken over by other institutions; as for, example, the fraternal group, the Jewish Center, or the community-wide fund-raising organization.

Perhaps the most significant change has not been in the structure of the synagogue, nor in its functions, but in the attitude of Jews toward religious services. Orthodox tradition requires that the Jew attend a synagogue for prayer three times a day, when this is physically possible. Conservative and Reform leaders do not object to this as an ideal, but many are willing to accept attendance at the Sabbath services as sufficient (Steinberg, 1947). Even this compromise is not always achieved. Our private conversations with religious leaders in several states indicated that synagogue or temple attendance is the rabbi's most pressing problem; sometimes securing a *minyan* (the minimum of ten males required before services can be held) when special services are to be held becomes an embarrassing problem.

What was the attitude of Jewish adolescents toward attendance at religious services? To answer this question we asked the respondents: "How often do you think Jews should go to temple or synagogue services?"

Only four per cent of the teenagers felt that Jews should attend services at least once a day; 44 per cent would be satisfied with attendance at Sabbath services; 38 per cent stated that only attendance at high holy day services was important; and 12 per cent did not believe that any attendance at religious services was necessary; two per cent left the question unanswered.

By traditional standards the frequency of religious service attendance of adolescents in the study was not high. Only 17 per cent of the Nebraska and Philadelphia group said they attended services "at least once a week," 26 per cent reported attendance "at least once a month," while the largest group, 55 per cent, went even less frequently, usually only on the high holy days. However, only 2 per cent reported no attendance at all. The question was put somewhat differently to the Yorktown group, but their responses were, on the whole, quite similar to the other samples: 12 per cent said they attended religious services "most Sabbaths," 36 per cent "some Sabbaths and high holy days," and 52 per cent "only on the high holy days, or less."

A Final Comment

In this and the previous chapter, we have examined the attitudes of Jewish adolescents towards certain traditional religious beliefs and practices and the degree to which adolescents observe them. Obviously, these beliefs and practices do not make up more than a fraction of the body of traditional Judaism. We need only note that it required five volumes to translate into English Joseph Albo's *Book of Principles* (1898), the definitive compilation of traditional Judaism's numerous beliefs, practices and customs, to realize how much more there is to traditionalism than we have been able to cover. It was never our goal, however, to survey the entire traditional doctrinal scene. Rather we have sought to examine those aspects of traditional practice and belief which the adolescents themselves regard as central to religion, even though the theologian may not agree with their point of view. We were, moreover, interested in those aspects of traditional Judaism which are especially sensitive, as we shall see, to majority and minority group influences as they are mediated through the various groups, large and small, formal and informal, to which the adolescent belongs. This being the central concern of this study, we turn now to an examination of the theoretical framework in which our data on group pressures and influences will be interpreted.

Attitude and Behavior Formation as a Function of Reference Groups

Attention so far has been focused primarily on a presentation of opinions held by the teenagers and a description of their behavior. Essentially, this has been in answer to the interrogative "What?"; that is, what do young people think and do about certain traditional religious beliefs and practices? It is now time to consider the more interesting but more difficult question of "Why?" By this we mean, why do adolescents accept some traditional religious tenets? Why do they reject others in whole or part? In short, what factors shaped the religious attitudes and behavior displayed by the youngsters in these samples?

The data collected in this study throw some light on the problem. In the following pages we shall outline a portion of the theoretical framework within which the data will be interpreted. Other elements in the theoretical framework will be presented in later sections containing the relevant data.

45

form of parents or parent-surrogates. These persons are of crucial importance to the child, who is dependent upon them for his very survival. However, since the very young child does not possess the linguistic tools necessary to the development of a social attitude he cannot be said to have significant referents.

As he grows older the child develops a more persistent and structured orientation toward the world about him. Once he becomes capable of social attitudes, significant others may become referents for behavior and attitude formation. During childhood referents are found for the most part at the primary level; that is, they are likely to be members of small, face-to-face groups such as the child's family or play group.

In addition to primary groups, the individual in complex societies ordinarily belongs to secondary groups as well — large, more impersonal collectivities or social aggregates. These groups are of relatively little importance to the young child, but with increasing age the individual participates more and more in secondary groups. By the time he is an adolescent their values and norms come to play a considerable role in determining his attitudes and behavior.

Groups may also be thought of as either ascribed or achieved (Linton, 1936). In the former, membership is involuntary and is usually attributed to the individual at birth. A good example of this is ethnic or national group membership. Achieved membership in a group, on the other hand, is a product of the person's own effort. An example of this type is membership in some fraternal or honorary association.

These distinctions between different types of groups have an important bearing on this study, for like most people Jewish adolescents belong, or aspire to belong, to a number of groups — primary and secondary, ascribed and achieved. Often these groups are highly alike in their orientations and expectations, but at times the norms and frames of reference of one group may conflict with those of another. The problems which this situation presents will be examined in a later part of this volume when the conflicts multiple group membership creates for the Jewish adolescent are discussed.

Sometimes a person consciously adopts a group's norms and expectations as his own; at other times they are learned before the individual is aware of his group membership, as is often the case in ascribed groups. But once the individual, for whatever reason, accepts its norms as his own, the group, whether it be primary or secondary, ascribed or achieved, becomes an effective agent in shaping values, attitudes and behavior. When the group performs this function we shall call it a "reference group."

THE REFERENCE GROUP CONCEPT

The term "reference group" was coined by Herbert Hyman and first appeared in his important monograph "The Psychology of Status" (1942). Despite its relatively recent origin the term has already acquired two distinctly different meanings. As the concept was used by Hyman, a reference group signifies some social category with which the individual compares himself in evaluating his own status. Essentially, in this usage the reference group operates as a model with which the person compares himself. Thus, in Hyman's study subject number 30, in evaluating her economic status, "realistically compared herself with groups who have what she desires. Her reference group for economic status consisted of friends who lived alone. Subject states she desires a career."

The term reference group has also been applied to a group whose norms provide frames of reference which effectively influence the attitudes and behavior of an individual. Muzafer Sherif (1948), who has used the concept extensively, defined it in this fashion:

"The place and functional meaning of the individual's social attitudes, belongingness (identification), and status aspirations and strivings become more real if they are related to groups from which they are derived. In other words, the individual's standards, attitudes, and status aspirations stem from and are related to certain groups. We shall refer to these groups as the individual's *reference* groups."[1]

Used in this way, the reference group *operates as an opinion leader and censor,* whose power to withhold approval or express disapproval enables it to enforce its norms as legitimate frames of reference for attitudes and behavior.

Considerable work in the study of groups has been done using the concept of reference group as censor and opinion leader, although social researchers have only recently begun to study attitudes explicitly in these terms, as Merton's (1957) and Shibutani's (1961) assessment of the literature on reference groups reveals. Thus, several early empirical studies of juvenile delinquency and neighborhood gangs (Thrasher, 1927; Shaw, 1938; Whyte, 1943) are excellent research examples of the impact of the primary group frame of reference upon the person. These studies showed how the need for belongingness and status, the pressure to conform, the need for group approval and the fear of disapproval operate to exact from the individual attitudes and behavior in keeping with the group's norms and values. On occasion the reference group may serve as both a model and censor-opinion leader, as Merton and Kitt (1950), in their analysis of the American Soldier data, have shown.

But it is a mistake to assume that reference groups always serve these functions simultaneously and that both are interchangeable elements of the same concept. Individuals or groups which serve as models for self-appraisal are not necessarily reference groups for one's attitudes. Consider the case of an individual who describes himself as a very poor card player. He compared himself with certain of his relatives who play cards

[1] Muzafer Sherif, *An Outline of Social Psychology,* New York: Harper, 1948, p. 105.

with considerable skill and enjoyment, but he neither enjoys card games nor regards them as a profitable way to spend leisure time. If asked to explain this attitude he might say that his parents rarely play cards, that his friends both past and present seldom play cards, and that in the social milieu in which he moves card playing is often regarded as the behavior of people too poor in ideas to make conversation.

This is an illustration of the common sense observation that an individual need not want to be like the person or group with which he compares himself. One group is used as a model for self-appraisal, and quite another one as a source of attitudes. Of course, the same person or group may, and frequently does, serve as a reference group for both self-appraisal and attitude formation. Probably this happens when the attribute involved in the comparison is important to the individual. That is to say, if the characteristic being compared (e.g., beauty, religiosity, card skill) is of sufficient value to the individual so that its presence or absence affects his self-esteem, then the other person or group involved in the comparison is likely to be a significant referent for attitude formation.

Now, our data show that most adolescents assigned a positive value to religion. In response to the question, "Is religion important to you?" 86 per cent of Yorktown's teenagers said "yes." When asked how important, 37 per cent said religion was very important, 58 per cent said it was moderately important, and 5 per cent told us it was only "slightly" important. This verbal "yea saying" to religion, it should be noted, did not coincide in many respects with actual behavior. Still, the very large percentage of adolescents who gave positive responses to the above question suggests that religion was a value for many teenagers, if only to the extent that many felt religion *should* be important to them.

Given this data, we expected to find a positive association between the teenager's model referents in religious matters and his attitude referents. Indeed, such an association did exist.

For example, when adolescents who said they were comparing themselves with an individual were asked whether this person had influenced their attitudes toward religion in any way, 58 per cent answered that they had. And to anticipate somewhat the data presented in the next section of this chapter, we found that many adolescents were using the same referents as models in religious self-estimations and as opinion leader-censors in attitude and behavior formation. This was especially likely to be the case when parents or age-mates were designated as significant referents. In most cases, teenagers who named their parents or peers as models in the assessment of their religiosity, also described them as influencing to a significant extent their religious attitudes and behavior.

THE RELIGIOUS SELF-ESTIMATION
AND THE REFERENCE GROUP

Every adolescent in this study was asked how religious he considered himself: very religious, moderately, slightly, or not at all religious. In addition, teenagers in Yorktown were asked whether their religious self-estimation involved a comparison with some person or group. We hoped that the search for models employed in religious self-estimation would also help us locate the referents for the adolescent's religious attitudes and behavior.

The concept of self-estimation, as it is understood here, involves a perception of some aspect of one's behavior and attitudes in comparison with others. There may be overtones of self approval or disapproval in self-estimations, though this is not always the case. An individual may be aware that he is a very poor dancer without this evaluation upsetting the satisfactory self-image he may have of himself. Self-estimations are segmentalized; the sum total of all self-estimations plus affective evaluative assessments make up the self-image, but any particular self-estimation should not be confused with the total self-image, nor need it necessarily be an important element in that self-image.

The religious self-estimation, then, involves a comparison of the individual with someone or something. But in order to understand how the adolescent arrived at a particular self-estimation, we need to know with whom or what he is comparing himself. Who are his models? Are they intimates or strangers? Are they individuals or groups? Fortunately, the Yorktown data enables us to provide some answers to these questions.

Individual Models

Somewhat less than half of the sample said their self-estimation involved a comparison with others; almost all listed individuals as models. Most teenagers named only one model, although a few named two or three. The individuals most often described as religious models were members of the respondent's family: their parents, grandparents, aunts or uncles. Members of the adolescent's peer group were the next most likely to serve as models. Some teenagers named their friends; others listed peers with whom they were not especially friendly but whose religiosity was well known.

Perhaps surprisingly, only a few teenagers listed the institutionalized bearers of religious traditions (e.g., the rabbi, the cantor, or the religious teacher) as models. Historically, these are the people who served as models for the entire community. Possibly, the religious standards they represented were so exacting that adolescents found comparisons with institutionalized bearers too invidious. At any rate, only one adolescent compared himself with his rabbi.

Group Models

A small number of adolescents said explicitly that they compared themselves with groups, not individuals. Most of these respondents said that they were comparing themselves with their friends, not any particular peer, but with the entire peer group evaluated as a whole. Only three respondents said that they were comparing themselves with the adult community. This would seem to agree with Hyman (1942), who found that total populations rarely figured as estimation models for his subjects.

Usually respondents compared themselves with their own membership groups, but this was not always the case. One boy, a temple member, compared himself with the entire synagogue membership. "I've never thought about it much," he said, "but I guess I'm comparing myself with the synagogue crowd. They seem to be more religious than I am." Then he added, smiling, "I guess I'm not much interested in religion." One girl, a synagogue member held in awe by her friends because she rarely missed Friday night services, said she was comparing herself with temple members. Her scorn for these people was vast, comparable only to her satisfaction with her own status. "You would hardly know they are Jews," she told us, "They've taken everything out of the religion. I don't see why they consider themselves Jews."

Conceptualized Models

About 40 per cent of the subjects denied that their self-estimation involved a comparison with anyone or anything. But when they were asked: "How did you get the idea that you are strongly religious, moderately religious, etc?" it was found that they were estimating their religiosity against a standard of performance explicit in the orthodox tradition.

Earlier, we noted that Jewish teenagers, regardless of denomination, defined religion in terms of traditional practices and beliefs. Traditionalism, as they understood it, involved a rigidly disciplined form of behavior which has become relatively rare in contemporary American society. It is improbable that the orthodox behavior which they employed in their description of religiosity was common in the world about them. In Yorktown, half of the youngsters came from homes in which non-kosher meat was used, while 36 per cent of their parents attend synagogue services only on the High Holy Days, and all but one family head worked on the Sabbath. This was certainly not a highly traditional community as the adolescents themselves defined the term.

Although many respondents said they knew of some person whose behavior fitted their description of strong religiosity, only infrequently was this a person whom they knew personally. Thus, for a number of the teenagers traditional beliefs and practices represented the standards of people whose existence was imperfectly known or merely postulated. Hyman calls this group a conceptual reference group. The sentiments and standards of a conceptual reference group are not those of actual persons with whom the respondent is acquainted. Indeed, the conceptual reference group may be composed of people long dead, or even legendary, who embody the heroic ideals and norms of a particular culture.

This leads us to the problem of "anchors," since the conceptual reference group was one of the anchors used by many adolescents in estimating their religiosity.

The Anchor Reference Group

All self-estimations implicitly involve anchors. People are only rich, ugly, intelligent, relative to the richness, ugliness or intelligence of other persons or things, and estimates of one's possession of these characteristics will vary with the referent used as an anchor. The factory worker who earns $6000 a year may consider himself fantastically wealthy if he uses the Chinese coolie as a referent; on the other hand, his income will seem paltry if he compares himself with the Rockefellers. Anchors are referents at the ends of the scale of comparison; they limit the space within which other intermediate referents may be located. Most anchors, however, tend not to be as extreme as these illustrations.

We have already noted that many of the adolescents were in effect comparing themselves with ideal traditional norms implicitly held by postulated referents. In a sense, these referents form an almost legendary community in which everyone is unflinchingly orthodox, synagogues are full on the sabbath and the dietary code is carefully observed. In short, not a world with which the adolescent is likely to have had any contact, for this type of community has all but disappeared in the United States. Nonetheless, it is this group which formed the upper anchor for almost all of our respondents.

Zangwill (1919) painted a vivid picture of an ideal member of the thoroughly orthodox community that serves as an upper anchor for many adolescents today.

> "In a land of *froom* men he was the *froomest* . . . . On the Sabbath he spoke nothing but Hebrew whatever the inconvenience and however numerous the misunderstandings, and if he perchance paid a visit he would not perform the "work" of lifting the knocker. Of course, he had his handkerchief girt round his waist to save him from carrying it, but this compromise being general was not characteristic of Karlkammer any more than his habit of wearing two gigantic sets of phylacteries where average piety was content with one of moderate size.

> One of the walls of his room had an unpapered and unpainted scrap in mourning for the fall of Jerusalem. He walked through the streets to the synagogue attired in his praying-shawl and phylacteries, and knocked three times at the door of God's house when he arrived. On the Day of Atonement he walked in his socks, though the heavens fell, wearing his grave-clothes. On this day he remained standing in the synagogue from 6 A.M. to 7 P.M. with his body bent

at an angle of ninety degrees; it was to give him bending space that he hired two seats."[2]

The use of an idealized traditional group, or its norms, as a referent for comparison is quite explicit in the explanations many of our respondents gave for their religious self-estimations. For example, one 16-year-old girl told us somewhat shame-facedly,

"If I was really religious, if I was a good Jew, I would keep *all* the rules. I wouldn't eat *tref* even if all the girls did. When I was younger I wouldn't ride on Saturday, but now . . . ." Then she added defiantly, "I don't abide by all the rules; I don't go to the synagogue, but I *do* keep the holidays."

A boy, who said he was moderately religious explained,

"Nobody's strongly religious anymore, see. It's a changing world; people don't have time for religion. I don't eat pork, and I go to the synagogue on Friday night sometimes, when the other fellows go. But I don't go regularly. I guess it wouldn't hurt me if I went more often."

The impact of this internalization of traditional norms on the adolescent can be seen in Tables 2 and 3. Treating the Nebraska and Philadelphia samples as one unit, it can be seen that the closer the teenager approaches the traditional norm the higher his religious self-estimation is likely to be. Thus, of the adolescents who said they never ate non-kosher food, 82 per cent described themselves as "strongly" or "moderately" religious, 18 per cent considered themselves to be "slightly" or "not at all" religious. The much larger group which reported eating non-kosher "often" gave much lower estimates of their religiosity: 36 per cent said they were strongly or moderately religious,

[2] Israel Zangwill, *Children of the Ghetto*, New York: Macmillan, 1919, pp. 146–147.

TABLE 2

Relationship Between Adolescent's Religious Self-Estimation and the Frequency of His Use of Non-Kosher Food

Adolescent Describes Himself As	Frequency of Use of Non-Kosher Food		
	Never PER CENT	Sometimes PER CENT	Often PER CENT
Strongly or Moderately Religious	82	65	36
Slightly or Not at all Religious	18	35	64
Total Number of Cases§	32	224	544

§ Not including adolescents who left a question unanswered.

This relationship is statistically significant at the .01 level as determined by a chi-square test.

TABLE 3

Relationship Between Adolescent's Religious Self-Estimation and the Frequency of His Religious Service Attendance

Adolescent Describes Himself As	Frequency of Religious Service Attendance		
	Weekly PER CENT	Monthly PER CENT	High Holy Days Only or Never PER CENT
Strongly or Moderately Religious	75	53	34
Slightly or Not at all Religious	25	47	66
Total Number of Cases§	136	208	456

§ Not including adolescents who left a question unanswered.

This relationship is statistically significant at the .01 level as determined by a chi-square test.

while 64 per cent described themselves as slightly or not at all religious.

Ritual observance has always been a salient element in religious self-estimation among Jews, but for the American adolescent it tends to be the only factor of any importance. Although Judaism is a system of beliefs and ethical concepts as well as practices, only traditional practices seem to be important in determining the adolescent's estimation of his religiosity as well as the religiosity of others. Adolescents were aware, of course, that Judaism possesses a body of beliefs and ethics: we were told that a religious person must believe in God, and that he should behave ethically. But being religious was not perceived as being *necessarily* ethical or "good." On more than one occasion a teenager would describe an individual whose behavior they found reprehensible but whom they considered highly religious because of his close adherence to the traditional norms of ritual observance. As we noted earlier this emphasis upon ritual observance is typical among adolescents irrespective of their denominational affiliation. Even adolescents affiliated with a Reform congregation estimated their religiosity within the traditionalistic frame of reference, despite the fact a majority of the traditional rituals have been discarded by Reformed Judaism.

At the other end of the continuum are the lower anchor referents, persons or groups the individual considers less religious than himself. Adolescents in this study were more likely to designate groups than individuals as lower anchors. For some synagogue youths the lower anchor was the "Temple Crowd." For others, atheists or "just Jews" (i.e., people who possess Jewish identity but are non-religious) served as lower anchors. But even though the group or individual chosen might vary somewhat from person to person, lower anchors possess one common characteristic which makes them recognizable in any context: they are always held in low esteem. Lower anchors are essentially the people or groups of whom one says, somewhat self-righteously, "At least, I'm not one of them!"

The Intermediate Reference Group

In arriving at a self estimate most people ordinarily compare themselves not only with anchor referents, but also with persons who more closely approximate their own status.

Thus, we found that while teenagers tended to compare themselves with persons more religious than themselves, these persons were not only ideal referents; intimate others in their family or peer group were also included. Of those who said they were comparing themselves with some individual about 7 out of 10 said that their referents were either parents, other close relatives, or age-mates.

In order to understand how the individual arrives at a particular self-estimate, it is important to recognize this interaction of anchor and intermediate referents in the self-estimation process. If respondents compared themselves only with their anchor-referents, which we know to be the ideal traditional group and its norms in most cases, it would be impossible to explain why so many respondents considered themselves even moderately religious. Compared to the ideal traditional standard, the behavior and attitudes of most teenagers in this study were virtually irreligious. Enough of the adolescents displayed a sufficiently adequate knowledge of traditional rituals and beliefs to make it difficult to see how so many could have contrasted that knowledge with their own behavior and still come to the conclusion that they were moderately religious, rather than "not religious at all" or at best "slightly religious."

The concept of *intermediate referent* suggests an answer to this problem. Intermediate referents are most likely to be members of the individual's family and/or peer group whose religiosity more closely approximates the respondent's own religious status. As we shall soon see, the religiosity of many adolescents reflected rather closely the standards and behavior of their families and peer groups. A comparison with others in the individual's own social milieu tempered his religious self-estimation. He saw his own behavior relative to that of friends, parents and his entire social circle. In this light, how he acted and what he thought did not appear so non-religious.

Still, if the ideal traditional standard were not an upper anchor-referent, if the respondent's parents and friends were *both* upper anchor and intermediate referents, there would be no reason why their self-estimations should be as modest as they often are. Why should so few adolescents consider themselves strongly religious? The answer, at least in part, is that the tendency of many adolescents to use the "heroic" traditional group (or actual persons whose behavior comes closest to approximating the traditional ideal) made it almost impossible for the adolescent to rate his religiosity very high; the traditional standards were much too exacting for most adolescents. Thus, only four per cent of the subjects felt that they were strongly religious, 42 per cent answered that they were moderately religious, 49 per cent only slightly religious, and five per cent said they were not religious at all.

The religious self-estimation, then, for most adolescents appears to be a product of comparisons with an upper anchor, intermediate referents and a lower anchor. The individual compares himself with an ideal code, the behavior of his family and friends, the actual social norms of the community and usually with some person or group which he believes to be less religious than himself.

The impact of the group upon the individual's religious self-estimation is very apparent in these data; and clearly it makes a difference which group the adolescent chooses as a model. But what about the effect of the group upon the teenager's religious convictions and conduct? What groups are important in this area, and how effective are they in molding the adolescent's religiosity? We know that the family and peer group often serve as models for religious self-estimations. Are they also reference groups for adolescents when it comes to religious beliefs and conduct? These are some of the questions to which we shall address ourselves in the following two chapters. Let us begin by examining the role of the family as a reference group.

The Family

No group is more influential in shaping the early attitudes and behavior of individuals in our society than the family. The reason for this can be found in the family's strategic contribution to early socialization — essentially a process during which the individual learns the behavior patterns, values and norms considered important by the groups to which he belongs. The critical importance of the family for socialization is primarily a function of certain distinctive characteristic which it alone possesses.

It is in the family that the individual first makes contact with the social world. Hence, familial agents of socialization are able to affect the child when he is most plastic and susceptible to social influence. The family is the group in which the individual first experiences the pleasures of affection and acceptance, learns the meaning of authority and control and develops a sense of identification with other human beings (Davis, 1950). The family, moreover, is perhaps the most enduring primary group to which the individual will ever belong. In a fast changing, mobile society, membership in groups is often unstable, altering as the individual assumes new roles or moves to new places. But even in our highly mobile society, parents and children try to stay in contact with one another in an attempt to keep a feeling of family identity alive (Goode, 1963).

Early in the socialization process, the child comes in contact with many of the norms and values of his society, primarily through the mediation of his parents, who act as instruments for the transmission of culture and the maintenance of socially acceptable attitudes and behavior. The family, however, is more than a mere instrument of transmission, uncritically communicating to the child whatever values, norms and attitudes society regards as desirable. Rather, it acts as a sort of filter that permits only selected aspects of the culture to reach the child. This selective process undoubtedly reflects the biases and predilections of the parent and may prevent the child from adopting ideas which his parents oppose (Murphy, 1947). Given the importance of the family in the socialization process, and recognizing the selective manner in which it transmits culture, it is not surprising that many people assume that children will share the attitudes of their parents and even retain the attitudes acquired in childhood throughout their lives.

Social scientists in their studies of attitudes have been quick to recognize the importance of the family. As early as 1937, Newcomb and Svehla reported positive correlations between children and parents in religious attitudes, attitudes toward communism and toward war. Hirschberg and Gilliland (1942) gave the same Thurstone scales to 200 undergraduates, aged 16–25, and found a low average parent-child correlation for attitude towards God. On the other hand, Allport, Gillespie and Young (1948) found that two-thirds of the Harvard students in their survey had reacted against their parents' religious views, at the age of approximately 15.

The underlying assumption of these studies is that the home is a religious attitude and behavior building agency. It is in the home that the child typically makes his first sustained contact with religion. If he is a Jewish child in an observant home, he learns that certain things are permissible and that others are taboo. By listening to his parents' conversation and observing their actions he learns about the food laws, proper conduct in the synagogue or temple, the meaning of the holy days and the Sabbath.

It must not be assumed, of course, that the home necessarily molds positive attitudes towards religion. A home which is passively non-religious, or in which the parents are openly hostile to traditionalism or to religion in general, may transmit negative attitudes toward specific practices or toward any aspect of religion. Even an observant home, especially a very traditional one in a generally non-traditional community, may cause the child to react against traditionalism. This was a common phenomenon a generation ago among youngsters from families in which the parents were first generation East European immigrants. This reaction is still occurring, as we shall see when the subject of parent-youth cross-pressures is examined in the following chapter.

Hollingshead's (1949) study, *Elmtown's Youth,* merits special notice for its emphasis on adolescence and its careful treatment of the family's role in the formation of teenage religious attitudes. Hollingshead wrote,

"Young Elmstowners acquire religious beliefs from their parents in the same way they learn that the parental home is their home. If the parents are devout Catholics, the children are introduced into the ritual and instruction of the church very early in life. Likewise a good Methodist family imparts to its children the traditional attitudes and beliefs in Methodism; or if the family is Methodist by tradition and not by practice, the children may be told that they are Methodists, but their connection with the local church may be tenuous. . . . Thus the young child has no more choice in the matter of religious beliefs than he does in the language he learns or the bed in which he sleeps. Finally, as is well known, religious attitudes learned at home are carried unconsciously into the neighborhood, the school, and other areas of community life."[1]

The statement "children acquire religious beliefs from their parents" translated into the language of reference group theory would read, "parents are religious referents for their children." But is such a translation worthwhile? Not if reference group theory required nothing more than the rephrasing of a simple declarative statement into the more technical language of social science. Fortunately, reference group theory does much more than this. Reference group theory states that the individual's attitudes and behavior are influenced by the expectations and example of significant others — persons or groups whose norms and values he has internalized. It reminds us that something more than a positive correlation between the attitudes of the parent and the attitudes of the child is needed as evidence before we can assert that a youngster's religious beliefs were indeed acquired from his parents. For strictly interpreted, a correlation between two sets of beliefs tells us nothing beyond the fact that the sets of beliefs are similar. Other data are necessary before a legitimate causal nexus can be inferred from a positive correlation between parent-child attitudes and behavior. Reference group theory alerts us to the importance of these data by re-

[1] August B. Hollingshead, *Elmtown's Youth,* New York: Wiley, 1949, p. 243.

quiring answers to certain crucial questions. Among these questions, the following will be examined in this chapter,

1. Does the adolescent perceive his parents as significant others? For example, are they persons whose opinion matters to the adolescent? Does he turn to them for advice?

2. Does he perceive the parent as influencing his religious attitudes and behavior? That is, are they religious referents?

3. What is the relationship between the adolescent's perception of what his parents expect of him as far as religion is concerned and (a) his religious attitudes and behavior, (b) his own religious self-expectations?

Obviously the search for answers to these questions requires a fuller exploration of the parent-adolescent relationship than would ordinarily occur if only the correlation between parent and child attitudes were studied. For in examining the influence of the parent upon the adolescent's attitudes and behavior, reference group theory requires that we consider the attitudes of parents and child *toward one another* as well as toward some substantive area.

The Parent as Significant Other

When used in studying adolescent attitudes and behavior, reference group theory requires an answer to this basic question: Of the many people with whom the adolescent has contact, which ones are important to him? One way of approaching this problem is to put the question to the adolescent himself. Teenagers in Yorktown were asked: "Think for a minute of the people whose opinion of you matters a great deal to you. Would you mind telling me their names?" Each interviewee was permitted to list as many people as he thought necessary. About nine out of ten respondents named one or both of their parents. In almost every case a parent was the first person to be mentioned. Younger respondents were especially apt to list parents, usually with a deprecatory smile which seemed to say, "Of course my parents are important to me. It's so obvious that it seems silly to mention it."

Other members of the immediate family were also named: 22 per cent mentioned their brothers or sisters; 12 per cent listed their grandparents; and 22 per cent named some aunt, uncle, or in-law.

In an effort to narrow the range of possible significant others and as a means of checking on the first question, we asked our subjects this question, "When you are trying to make up your mind about something important, whose ideas do you pay the most attention to?" Once again the parent appeared most often in the adolescent's reply: 84 per cent named their mother, 80 per cent named their father, while 26 per cent turned to a brother, and 20 per cent to a sister. The modal number of persons listed in answer to this question was two, half the number listed for the previous question.

Thus the answers to both questions strongly indicate that teenagers regard their parents as important people in their lives. This finding is hardly surprising; it is a commonplace assumption and was, of course, anticipated in our examination of the family's role in the socialization process.

The Parent as Religious Referent

Now, as we already know, significant others are not necessarily referents in every situation. Hence, we could not assume that parents were *religious* referents even though their perceived general importance was great. We felt it was necessary to probe further for religious referents; we began by asking this question: "Think for a minute of all the people who have helped make you feel the way you do about religion. Would you mind telling me their names?"

It was evident from their answers that teenagers place a large share of the responsibility for their attitudes towards religion on their parents. Eighty-four per cent named their father and 88 per cent named their mother as persons who had influenced them in religious matters. Often adolescents, particularly those from traditionalistic homes, would attribute their observance of some religious practice to parental influence. These influences, as the youngsters perceived them, can be roughly divided into three groups.

(1) *Habituation:* Frequently an adolescent would trace his observance of some ritual to a habit formed in the home. For example, one 17-year-old boy stated that he intended to observe *kashruth* in his home when married because,

> "I'm used to it. *We always kept kosher in our home.* I don't know — it just seems the right thing to do. It's the way my parents taught me."

(2) *Affection:* In many cases the adolescent observed a certain ritual not from personal preference but in deference to his parents. Often the youngster was motivated by affection for his parents. He was prepared to sacrifice his own desires to please them. Thus, a 15-year-old girl told us she would "keep a *kosher* home" against her own or even her prospective spouse's preference because,

> "I don't want to hurt my parents. I know they would never come to eat in my house if I didn't keep *kosher*. I don't believe in it myself — some of it is so stupid — but it means a lot to them."

(3) *Coercion:* Only a few adolescents felt they had been coerced into observing some particular practice through fear of parental retribution. However, several adolescents in Philadelphia believed that their parents would, as one girl put it, "hit the ceiling if I ate *chomutz*. Whenever I go out they want to know what I ate. *Pesach* (Passover) is like a prison sentence for me."

Parents do not hold quite so strong a position as a religious referent as they do in the role of general significant other. In religious matters parents compete with the rabbi and the religious teacher — persons who do not figure at all as significant others in the everyday life of the adolescent. Thirty per cent of our subjects named their rabbi, and 22 per cent their religious teacher as persons who had influenced their attitudes toward religion. Neither of these two referents had been named by the adolescent as persons whose opinion of them mattered. We might note as an aside that this is in rather sharp contrast to the situation in earlier Jewish communities where the prestige of the rabbi made him an important factor in many areas of adolescent life.

Every adolescent was asked, in addition, "Have they (the people who influenced you) tended to make you more religious or less religious?"

Most of the respondents felt that their referents had tended to make them *more* religious. All but two teenagers said their mothers' influence had helped make them more religious; about two-thirds believed their fathers had tended to keep them interested in religion and in some cases to make them even more religious.

The Expectations of Parents

Significant referents have been defined as persons whose expectations and norms are internalized by another individual. If parents are significant referents, as seemed likely, we should be able to find a marked relationship between the expectations of the parent and the behavior and attitudes of the child.

The data obtained from several questions in the interview schedule made possible an examination of this relationship. Interviewees in Yorktown were asked: "As far as religion is concerned, what do your parents expect of you?" Their answers were placed in one of four categories, depending upon the parents' definition of religion and the specificity of parental expectations.

(1) *Ritual Observance*

Some parents (34 per cent), all of them members of the Orthodox congregation, defined religion in terms of ritual practice and observance. These parents stressed the observance of traditional practices, particularly the dietary laws and Sabbath synagogue attendance. The latter two demands were the most stringent placed upon the adolescent. A typical comment from adolescents in this group was the following remark made by a 15-year-old girl,

> "They want me to keep as many things as I can, to keep *kosher* if possible, and not to eat things I'm not supposed to both in and out of the house. They'd like me to go to *Shul* on Friday night. Of course I have to go on the high holidays; they won't let me go to school on the Jewish holidays."

(2) *Diffuse Positive Orientation Toward the Group*

A few parents (eight per cent) apparently defined religion as a feeling of group belongingness. They asked only that their children maintain an active awareness of their ethnic identity and do nothing to jeopardize it. These parents were primarily concerned about intermarriage; they encouraged their children to "remember they are Jews," to maintain some contact with other Jewish adolescents and to avoid dating those of other faiths. As one 16-year-old boy put it,

> "My parents don't expect me to be religious. They are not religious themselves, but they want me to be with Jewish kids some of the time. They like it when I go down to the Center. Most of my friends aren't Jewish, you know. I come down here mostly to please my parents."

(3) *Diffuse Positive Orientation Toward Religion*

A large proportion of the parents (52 per cent) placed only the vaguest, most general demands upon their children. These parents felt that some contact with religion was worthwhile, but were rather unsure as to what that contact should be. They were much less concerned with the observance of religious practices than with the idea that the child somehow develop a generally positive attitude toward religion. The attitude of these parents is summed up in the following comment made by a 17-year-old girl,

> "My mother and father feel it's important that I have *some* religion. They expect me to do about the same thing they do, to know something about the religion, to know the customs."

(4) *Indifferent or Negative*

A small group of parents (six per cent) appeared to be either hostile to religion or entirely indifferent. Their children reported that they knew of no parental expectations with respect to religion. Respondents in this category were likely to tell us,

> "I don't know, never thought about it. I don't think they expect very much, I guess. Now that you mention it I don't think they ever talk about it, except once when we had some people over the house and they talked about those Jehovah people who stand on the street corner."

We used this classification of responses to construct an index of parental religious expectations. Parents (category 1) who stressed ritual observance (i.e., eating kosher meat or attending Friday evening services) will be regarded as having relatively traditionalistic expectations; parents (other categories) who expected only a diffuse positive orientation toward religion, or who expected only commitment to ethnic identity, or who expected nothing at all will be regarded as having non-traditionalistic expectations.

In order to compare parental expectations with the adolescent's level of religious traditionalism, three attitude and behavior scales were constructed from among a number of questions, already examined in earlier chapters, concerning traditional beliefs and practices.

A. Scale of Adolescent's Attitude toward Beliefs

A measure of attitude toward traditional beliefs was obtained from responses to questions about six beliefs: (1) a personal God, (2) the Torah as divine revelation, (3) reward and punishment after death, (4) the Messiah, (5) a historical and prophetic Moses, and (6) the doctrine that the Jews are a chosen people. Respondents who gave traditional responses to four or more of these questions will be considered as relatively traditionalistic.

B. Scale of Adolescent's Attitude toward Practices

This scale was obtained from responses to questions about four traditional practices: (1) the use of *kosher* food, (2) observance of the holy days, (3) synagogue or temple attendance, and (4) the emphasis placed upon religious study. Respondents who gave traditional responses to three or more of these questions will be considered relatively traditionalistic.

C. Scale of Adolescent's Religious Conduct

Two items were used to index the adolescent's level of traditional conduct: one dealing with the use of non-*kosher* food, the other with attendance at religious services. Adolescents who refrained from eating non-*kosher* food or who ate it only infrequently, and whose attendance at Sabbath services was regular will be considered as being relatively traditionalistic.

An analysis of scales A and B, using Lazarsfeld's (1949) latent structure method, revealed that they possessed a latent attribute which we defined as religious traditionalism.

We are now in a position to examine the relationship between parental expectations and adolescent religiosity. As can be seen in Table 4, there is a clear association between what parents expect and how the child thinks and behaves: the more traditionalistic the expectation level, the more likely it is that the adolescent will be traditionalistic in attitude and conduct. Thus 53 per cent of the adolescents whose parents had traditionalistic expectations were traditionalistic in attitude toward beliefs, 71 per cent in attitude toward practices and 59 per cent in behavior; whereas of those adolescents whose parents had non-traditionalistic expectations, only 15 per cent were traditionalistic in attitude toward beliefs, 21 per cent in attitude toward practices, and 9 per cent in behavior.

Conceivably the relationship between parental expectation and the child's religious attitude and behavior could be entirely a function of parental coercion. Adolescents, it may be argued, behave as they do because they must. But reference group theory requires that the relationship between the attitudes and behavior of the individual and the expectations of his referent be more than a function of his subordination to power and authority. If the parents are truly religious referents for the adolescent, parental expectations should not only influence his attitudes and behavior, they should affect his religious self-expectations as well.

Fortunately, the data permit us to examine the relationship between parental expectations and the adolescent's religious self-expectation. The question "Do you feel you ought to be more religious?" was used as an index of the adolescent's religious self-expectation. An answer "yes" can be interpreted as indicating that the respondent is not satisfied with his own level of performance and expects more of himself. The data in

TABLE 4

Relationship Between Parental
Religious Expectations and Adolescent's
Religious Attitudes and Behavior

	Parental Expectations of Adolescent Are	
	Traditionalistic PER CENT	Non-Traditionalistic PER CENT
Adolescent's Attitude Towards Beliefs		
Traditionalistic	53	15
Non-Traditionalistic	47	85
Adolescent's Attitude Towards Practices		
Traditionalistic	71	21
Non-Traditionalistic	29	79
Adolescent's Behavior		
Traditionalistic	59	9
Non-Traditionalistic	41	91
Total Cases	17	33

These relationships are statistically significant at the .01 level or better as determined by a chi-square test using Yates correction factor.

Table 5 show a marked relationship between parental expectations, as perceived by the adolescent, and his religious self-expectation. Adolescents who reported their parents as having relatively traditionalistic expectations were far more likely (82 per cent) to feel they ought to be more religious than adolescents (36 per cent) whose parents' expectations were non-traditionalistic.

This finding emphasizes an important theoretical contribution of reference group theory, for it makes possible an explanation

TABLE 5

Relationship Between Parental
Religious Expectation and Adolescent's
Religious Self-Expectation

Adolescent Feels He Ought To Be More Religious	Parental Expectations of Adolescent Are	
	Traditionalistic PER CENT	*Non-Traditionalistic* PER CENT
Yes	82	36
No	18	64
Total Cases	17	33

This relationship is statistically significant at the .01 level as determined by a chi-square test using Yates correction factor.

of a phenomenon which at first glance seems anomalous. One might expect that the teenager's religious self-expectations would be geared to his own level of traditional performance: the more traditionalistic the individual, the more likely he is to feel content with his religiosity. Yet the respondents who were most likely to express dissatisfaction with their level of religiosity were precisely those who were most traditionalistic. Using the framework of reference group theory, it would seem that the religious expectations of parents, as religious referents, had been internalized and employed by the adolescent in evaluating his own religious performance. The higher the standard implicit in parental expectations the more traditionalistic and exacting the expectations, the more difficult it becomes to satisfy the referent — and oneself. In Mead's (1934) terminology the adolescent has "taken the role of the other towards himself," and it would appear that the expectations of the referent played a more important role in the formation of religious self-expectations than the individual's own behavior.

Parental Behavior and Adolescent Religiosity

Parents, then, are perceived as religious referents whose expectations affect the adolescent's beliefs, conduct and self-expectations. We may proceed to examine the relationship between *what the parent does* and how the child behaves.

A *Scale of Parental Traditionalism* was constructed in the following manner. Adolescents were asked six questions about the degree to which their parents observed certain traditional practices. The questions concerned (1) the use of *kosher* food in the home, (2) the use of separate flesh and dairy cooking and eating utensils, (3) the lighting of candles on Friday evening, (4) cooking on the Sabbath, (5) parental religious service attendance, and (6) parental abstention from work on the Sabbath. Originally, we were concerned that obtaining these data from the adolescent rather than the parent might have introduced some error into the data, but later interviews with a number of parents indicated that the adolescents' reports were substantially correct. An analysis of these questions by Lazarsfeld's latent structure method revealed a latent attribute which we defined as religious traditionalism. For purposes of statistical analysis, we shall consider parents whose behavior is traditional in four or more of these practices as being relatively traditionalistic.

The Philadelphia, Yorktown and Nebraska samples were combined into one group and the level of parental traditionalism was then cross-tabulated with the adolescents' religious attitude and conduct, using the scales described earlier in this chapter. The data in Table 6 show that where parents were traditionalistic, the adolescents were also more likely to be traditionalistic — a finding in keeping with the notion that parents are important in shaping the religious attitudes and behavior of their children. Apart from this basic conclusion, however, there are several additional aspects of the data which merit further examination.

TABLE 6

Relationship Between Parental
Religious Traditionalism and the
Traditionalism of their Children

	Parents Are	
	Traditionalistic PER CENT	*Non-Traditionalistic* PER CENT
Adolescent's Attitude Towards Beliefs		
Traditionalistic	47	20
Non-Traditionalistic	53	80
Adolescent's Attitude Towards Practices		
Traditionalistic	58	17
Non-Traditionalistic	42	83
Adolescent's Behavior		
Traditionalistic	31	7
Non-Traditionalistic	69	93
Total Cases§	193	617

§ Not including adolescents who left a question unanswered. These relationships are statistically significant at the .01 level or better as determined by the chi-square test.

First, it should be noted that parent traditionalism is more closely associated with the adolescent's attitude toward practices than toward beliefs. Thus, of those adolescents whose parents were traditionalistic, 58 per cent were traditionalistic in attitude toward practices, 47 per cent in attitude toward beliefs. While this may be a function, in part at least, of the nature of the parental scale (the scale is composed entirely of ritual-oriented items), it probably also reflects the tendency of many traditionalistic parents to place much greater stress upon ritual observance than on beliefs.

Second, parental traditionalism is more closely related to traditionalism in the adolescent's attitudes than in his conduct: of those adolescents whose parents were traditionalistic, 58 per cent were traditionalistic in their attitude toward practices, only 31 per cent were traditionalistic in their actual behavior. Apparently, it is easier for the parent to shape the attitudes of the child than to influence his behavior, at least in this area.

Third, not every adolescent conformed to the parental point of view, despite the fact that a very large proportion of the adolescents perceived their parents as religious referents. Deviations from the parental pattern was greatest in cases where the parent was traditionalistic, possibly because the traditionalistic parent had fewer sources of support for his position in the general society, where the trend appears to be away from orthodoxy. Nonetheless, traditionalism in children was more common where the parents were traditional than when they were nontraditional.

The finding that some adolescents did not adopt the behavioral and attitudinal patterns of their referents — in this case their parents — points up a significant limitation of the reference group approach *when only one group is offered as an explanatory factor*. True, this approach prompts the researcher to collect data which make possible better subsubstantiated statements about the causal nexus between parent-child religious attitudes and conduct than would be possible if only the limited correlational approach was used. Thus, we began by showing that adolescents perceived their parents as significant others and religious referents. The data also revealed a significant relationship between parental expectations and adolescent self-expectation. We then went on to demonstrate the existence of an association between parent-child religious attitudes and behavior. These data consistently and cumulatively point to the parent as an important factor influencing the adolescent's religiosity.

Still, notwithstanding these findings, the number of adolescents who do not conform to parental expectations suggests that an understanding of so complex a phenomenon as religious behavior requires a research design which considers the possibility that not one but several significant groups may be acting upon the individual simultaneously (Rosen, 1959). Certainly, when studying adolescents, the researcher must be alert to the possibility that there may be referents of even greater significance to the youngster than his parents. For, while the family is clearly important in shaping many attitudes and behavior, it does not follow that the child will necessarily adopt every aspect of the parents' behavior or internalize all of their expectations. There are other influences in the child's life besides his parents. In the next chapter we shall examine one of the most important of these influences — the peer group.

C h a p t e r   S e v e n

The Peer Group

Adolescence has sometimes been described as a period in the life cycle typified by great psychic strain and emotional upheaval. The person initially responsible for this *Sturm und Drang* conception of adolescence was G. Stanley Hall (1905), a psychologist and educator, whose eclectic work on adolescence blended evolutionary theory, the facts of physical growth, instinct psychology and numerous references to ethnographic material to form a conception of adolescence as a stage of life in which a "rebirth of the soul" inevitably brought the adolescent into conflict with society.

This approach was later challenged by other social scientists. Anthropologists introduced evidence which revealed that adolescence in some primitive cultures was relatively free from strain, and that the passage of the individual from one status to another was made easy through explicit institutionalized mechanisms. Their studies indicated that adolescent conflicts, when they existed, were largely determined by cultural factors.

81

Gradually, with the increase of empirical information about the adolescent, the storm and stress conception of adolescence was considerably modified and the physiological and instinctivist premises upon which it was based were largely abandoned.

Although anthropologists and ethnographers have shown that strain and conflict are not everywhere associated with adolescence, there is considerable reason to believe that this period is one of turmoil and confusion in American society. This characteristic of adolescence is partly a product of the physiological changes which occur at this time. Also important are the culturally induced conflicts which American society creates for its adolescents.

Physiological changes produce a host of new problems for the adolescent; problems so numerous and vexing that some adolescents fear to grow up (Hollingsworth, 1928). Alterations in the physical organism and its functioning often lead to anxiety as to whether the changes are normal and desirable. Some adolescents view every change in body contour with apprehension. They feel unnatural as the childish form disappears and excessively conspicuous as they try to handle the new attributes of their body which increasing age has wrought.

Ranking high among the disturbing physiological factors in adolescence is the insistent urging of sex. At puberty, the sex organs undergo physiological changes which are accompanied by new feelings and tensions spurred by new social awarenesses. Responding to new powers and needs, the adolescent yearns to participate in activities which promise enjoyment and relief. But for many adolescents the fulfillment of his desires are frustrated by a salient characteristic of adolescence in American society — the lag between physical maturation and social maturity (Davis, 1950). In terms of growth, strength, fecundity and mental capacity full maturity tends to be attained in adolescence; socially, however, the individual may remain a child for many years after puberty. Though the adolescent is physically able to engage in sexual intercourse and is bombarded on all sides by the suggestive stimuli of popular culture, he is nonetheless expected to curb his sexual appetite and remain continent until marriage — in a society which discourages early marriage. Caught between such conflicting pressures, adolescents seem at times apathetic towards sex, at other times sex-ridden, insecure and apprehensive (Sullivan, 1947).

Sex is by no means the only ambiguous, unclear area for the adolescent. For example, American culture stresses self-reliance and independence as values and personality traits for individuals at almost all age levels. Adolescents cannot help but be aware of this. Yet adolescence remains a period of prolonged dependency, with far fewer areas of autonomy than adults enjoy and little activity which is functional for society as a whole and from which the adolescent can derive a sense of achievement. In our affluent society relatively few adolescents need make a serious contribution to their own support or to their family. They are encouraged to play and to indulge themselves. When they do so, in what to many parents seems an obsessive fashion, they are dismayed to discover that their parents consider this behavior childish. Wanting to grow up, the adolescent is encouraged to remain a child; behaving childishly, he is admonished to grow up. Is it any wonder that ofttimes he feels insecure, adrift in a world without guidelines, beset by conflicting expectations and frustrations.

In his effort to cope with the tensions which plague him, the teenager turns to his age-mates for companionship, recognition and support. Drawn to each other by mutual need, adolescents try to find comfort in their own sub-culture. They develop common interests and tastes in music, dancing and movies; they exchange confidences and create exotic symbols which they alone understand. In time, out of these common ties and mutually shared interests, there will often develop cliques with recognizable group properties, among which is the capacity to generate powerful norms and loyalties. Empirical studies (Gordon, 1957; Coleman, 1961) of the social sub-cultures which adolescents create show clearly how peer expectations and norms influence the adolescent's tastes, aspirations and values.

Among Jewish adolescents, the peer group is as important a factor in everyday life as it is among the general teenage population. Thus, when Yorktown teenagers were asked to name "the people whose opinion of you matters a great deal to you," 70 per cent included one or more of their age-mates. Almost a fourth of the adolescents interviewed said they would turn to one of their peers when making up their minds about something important. In the language of reference group theory, the adolescent generally regarded his peers as significant others. Yet, he tended not to perceive his peers as an important force affecting his religious attitudes and behavior. In other words, they were not perceived as religious referents. The idea that age-mates might influence him in this area seemed to most adolescents to be a bit bizarre. The family and the religious school, not his peer group, were the major factors shaping his religious attitudes and behavior — or so he believed. When Yorktown adolescents were asked to name "the people who helped make you feel the way you do about religion, only 18 per cent named a peer, while 88 per cent named one or both of their parents.

As sometimes happens, the gap between perception and reality proved to be very wide. Intensive interviewing and the observations of adolescents in Yorktown over a year's period revealed a situation quite different from what the adolescent believed to be the case. The peer group proved to be a far more potent factor than the adolescent imagined. In order to understand the manner and degree to which the peer group affected the adolescent in this area, it will be necessary to examine the formal and informal groups to which he belonged. By describing their general composition and distinctive characteristics, we shall be better able to understand how they influenced his religious attitudes and behavior. Let us begin by examining the formal youth groups in Yorktown.

The Formal Youth Groups

There were four formal Jewish youth groups in Yorktown at the time of the study: a boys' group and three girls' groups. These groups possessed several characteristics which have an important bearing upon our problem. For one thing, although their membership was exclusively Jewish there seemed to be little else that was "Jewish" about the groups. In the words of one adult informant, the clubs were only "nominally Jewish."

The most adult of the youth groups was a local chapter of Junior Hadassah, a girls' club with 18 members ranging in age from 17 to 22. Junior Hadassah was a Zionist group whose manifest function was to promote philanthropic projects in Israel. But, as its president told us with an apologetic smile, only a few of the girls in the Yorktown group were seriously interested in Zionism. Of course, periodic contributions were made to the Hadassah headquarters, but these seemed to be more in the nature of payments for the use of a highly regarded group name than a token of serious political and social convictions.

The principal though unexpressed function of the club was to provide social opportunities for the late adolescent and early adult Jewish girls in the community — no small task in a town where males were scarce and noticeably reluctant to date town girls. Characteristically, the most serious problem facing the club each Spring was not, as one might imagine from its name, the construction of a hospital or school in Israel, but the procurement of dates for the less enterprising girls in time for an important annual dance. An attempt had been made to institute a quasi-religious program, but at the time of the study it had aroused very little interest.

The most vigorous of the girls' groups was the Sorority, Tau Beta Sigma, with about twenty girls, ages 15 through 18, in the club. A large percentage of its members were active; its leaders were competent, and the competition for office was spirited. The group possessed an *élan* noticeably absent in the other formal groups. Unlike the other three youth groups, the sorority borrowed its prestige from Greek, not Jewish sources — not the first time Jews have shown an affinity for non-Jewish symbols in preference to their own. The sorority did not have even a nominal Jewish cultural or religious program. It was what it professed to be — a social club resembling other social clubs created to satisfy the social proclivities of its members.

The pre-adolescent and early adolescent girls (12 through 14 years of age) had their own club, with nine members. Apart from its name (Young Judea) and membership, it too seemed to be devoid of Jewish cultural or religious content. No one seemed at all certain about the goals or philosophy of the group. Some of its members had never heard of the parent national organization: the club's 14-year-old president thought that Young Judea was an affiliate of a national Zionist organization (it is), but she was not certain.

Its lack of goals, however, did not seem to bother the club; it was a happy, cohesive group with none of the internecine conflicts that plagued the older groups. The parents of the girls believed that the club served a valuable function in bringing the girls together in a Jewish environment (the Jewish Center), and affording them "social opportunities," that is, the chance to strike up friendships with other Jewish girls and to meet Jewish boys.

There was only one boys' group — an adolescent affiliate of B'nai Brith called Aleph Zadik Aleph. At the time of this study the local chapter seemed moribund. Of its 15 or so members less than half were active ones, and we never saw more than five at a meeting. A.Z.A., as it was called, was the only one of the four clubs which regarded itself as a religious group as well as a social club. Theoretically the group had a religious program, but it was never able to get it really started. A joint father-son religious service was discontinued after a few weeks when support from adults and adolescents alike proved insufficient. As the club's president put it, "A.Z.A. is more a social club than a religious one."

Another characteristic of the youth clubs was their non-exclusiveness. All Jewish teen-agers in Yorktown were not only urged to join a youth group appropriate to their age level, considerable pressure was placed upon them both by adults and other adolescents to do so, even in cases where the individual was clearly reluctant. There were basically two reasons for this situation. The first was pragmatic: the clubs needed members, and there were too few Jewish teen-agers in Yorktown to permit much selectiveness. If the clubs were to have sufficient members to carry on adequate social activities (dances, banquets, etc.) they had, as the sorority's president put it, "to try our hardest to get everyone to join! there are really so few girls." The second reason was a function of ethnic cohesiveness — the strong belief among Yorktown's Jewish teenagers that all Jewish teenagers *because they were Jewish* had a right as well as an obligation to belong to one of the Jewish clubs.

In addition, many parents actively encouraged their children to join some Jewish group, in part because they recognized that the community expected it of them, and in part out of a feeling that some contact with other Jewish adolescents was a "good thing."

Unfortunately for the youth groups, the policy of non-exclusiveness had several friction-producing consequences. In the case of the fraternity (A.Z.A.), it led to the inclusion of 13

and 14 year olds into the group, so that the club included boys
from 13 through 18 years of age. An 18 year old boy feels that
he has very little in common with a 13 year old. One of the
boys gave this as his reason for dropping out of the club. He
told us,

> "A.Z.A. used to be strong, but now it has petered out.
> They take in kids too young, even eighth graders. You can't
> have a fraternity with eighth graders and seniors. There's no
> fraternity feeling."

Nor was there any feeling of selectiveness; the non-exclusiveness policy robbed the groups of their prestige appeal. What
honor was there, an adolescent complained, in belonging to a
group which was open to all, regardless of merit or socio-
economic status?

The anomalous result of the policy of non-exclusiveness was
the heterogeneous character it introduced into groups that are
normally highly homogeneous. Members of every social category in Yorktown's Jewish community could be found in the
clubs. Yet the community was not as homogeneous as the
"middle class" label usually applied to it would suggest. There
were rich Jews in Yorktown and poor Jews, religious Jews and
atheists, synagogue members and temple members, West Siders
and East Siders, and so forth. Given the various pressures upon
the adolescent to join a youth group, the formal clubs became
in effect, primary groups characterized by compulsory interaction between adolescents from families with widely differing
statuses — a situation well calculated to create friction. Indeed,
friction did exist and on several occasions threatened to destroy
the clubs.

The Religious Influence of the Formal Groups

Jewish formal youth groups in Yorktown seemed to exert
little effect on the religious behavior and attitudes of their mem-

bers. The reasons for this should by now be apparent: the clubs (with the exception of Young Judea) suffered from interpersonal conflicts or were hampered by the apathy of many of their members; they had no serious religious orientation, no religious program, no religious goals. They were social clubs whose main distinctive feature was their ethnic composition. In most other respects, in program, outlook and structure, they resembled any number of non-Jewish youth groups in the city.

Yet, in a negative sense, the formal groups did affect the religious behavior of Jewish adolescents. For the formal groups, torn by dissension and weakened by member apathy, left a vacuum into which other groups could move. The need for support and direction which could not be satisfied through participation in formal clubs had to be taken care of in some other fashion; the informal group provided this service. Small, intimate aggregates of adolescents bound together by mutual needs and interests but without any preformulated program or organization, the informal group became a potent force in Yorktown's adolescent society. Undoubtedly they would have existed anyway, but the absence of significant countervailing influence from the formal groups greatly magnified their importance. Their impact upon the adolescent's religious conviction and conduct proved to be highly significant and much greater than most adult members of the Jewish community recognized.

THE INFORMAL YOUTH GROUPS

In some respects the Jewish teenagers of Yorktown formed one large peer group. Their number was sufficiently small so that they were all able to know one another, at least by name and face. In the synagogue or temple, at the Jewish Center or at school, the Jewish teenager continually interacted with other members of his ethnic group. He sometimes referred to other

Jewish adolescents as if they did in fact form a single group using such terms as "the Jewish kids" or "they" to describe some aspect of Jewish life in Yorktown, or even to explain his own behavior. But a group as heterogeneous as this is essentially unstable and will tend to break into smaller, more homogeneous clusters. This is precisely what occurred in Yorktown. The adolescents tended to cluster into small all-male or all-female groups whose members were closer in age and social class.

In order to locate these groups we asked the adolescents to list the persons among his age-mates, both Jewish and non-Jewish, "with whom you go around, the ones you are friendliest with." In addition, they were asked to describe how the other Jewish teenagers grouped themselves. These data were buttressed by information gained in Yorktown over a period of a year during which we were able to observe how and with whom the adolescents interacted in a variety of formal and informal situations. Through combining these diverse data it was possible to locate each adolescent in a peer group.

Jewish teenagers tended to choose their friends from among age and sex peers in the Jewish community: only five subjects listed more non-Jewish than Jewish friends. But the groups they formed varied greatly in cohesiveness. Among the younger adolescents, particularly the boys, group membership tended to be somewhat fluid; some of the boys moved from one group to another. At the other extreme were the older girls who tended to form tightly knit enduring groups. Two of these groups deserve some examination for though they were small in size — only three girls in each group — their solidarity and popularity were so great and their antipathy toward each other so strong that they divided the Jewish girls of Yorktown into two passively hostile factions.

One of the first things we were told about Yorktown was that it was "cliquey." One 16-year-old girl remarked that, "cliquing is the main problem in this town." The president of A.Z.A. confirmed this: he said, "There is a West Side clique and an East Side clique, and they don't mix too well."

Much of the tension between the two groups stemmed from differences in socio-economic status. The South Side clique and its hangers-on were daughters of less affluent, though by no means poor, members of the community. They resented the West Side girls, whom they accused of abusing their parents' wealth and position. We were told that "they (the West Side girls) feel that because their fathers have money they can do what they want." The South and East Side girls had so defined the situation that the West Side clique felt itself excluded; they knew that beneath the facade of sororal fellowship lay a good deal of hostility, and they responded with intense solidarity. The adult advisor of the sorority, who deplored the clique conflict, complained:

> "They come to meetings together; they sit together; they leave together. You can see it; you can feel it. If you put one of them on a committee, you have to put the others on it."

Without much question, the South Side clique was the victor in its internecine war with the West Side trio. Their popularity with the boys (two of them had "steady" boy friends), their activity in the sorority, and their personal attractiveness gave them considerable prestige. They were, in effect, the leaders of all the South and East Side girls.

The East Side-West Side schism was present among the boys to a lesser extent. It was not uncommon to find West Side, South Side and East Side boys at parties together. But in more formal settings friction sometimes arose. During one year in Yorktown, several of the West Side boys dropped out of the fraternity because they were unwilling to remain under the dominance of the numerically superior South Siders whose leadership, in their opinion, was "running A.Z.A. into the ground."

As we have already noted a major effect of this tension between groups was to weaken the formal organizations, make community-wide programs and activities more difficult and heighten the importance of personal influence within the informal peer group.

The Informal Peer Group and Religion

If the notion that the peer group is a powerful factor in the lives of adolescents is correct, one would expect to find, as a result of frequent interaction and exchange of ideas, a fairly high degree of similarity in their attitudes and behavior in a variety of areas. One of these areas could be religion, despite the adolescent's tendency to deprecate this possibility. The data indicate this to be the case.

Consider, for example, our findings on the similarity between the adolescent's attitude and that of his peers toward a single ritual practice of traditional Judaism — the use of *kosher* meat. As a way of putting the influence of the peer group in perspective, parent-adolescent attitude similarity in this area will also be presented. The position of the adolescent, his peers and his parents as regards this practice was determined by asking the subjects: "When you get married are you going to use *kosher* meat in your home?" and "Is *kosher* meat used in your home?" Adolescents who planned to use and parents who were using *kosher* meat will be considered observant. An examination was made of the attitudes of the members of each peer group; where more than half of the members said that they would follow this traditional practice when married, the group was considered observant.

As can be seen in Table 7, adolescents tend to have attitudes very similar to those of their peer group: for example, in four out of five cases where the group is observant the adolescent is

TABLE 7

*Relationship between the Attitude of Adolescents
Toward the Use of Kosher Food and the Attitude
of their Parents and Peer Group*

Adolescent's Attitude	Parental Attitude		Peer Group Attitude	
	Observant	*Non-Observant*	*Observant*	*Non-Observant*
	PER CENT		PER CENT	
Observant	60	32	80	23
Non-Observant	40	68	20	77
Total Cases	25	25	20	30

These relationships are statistically significant at the .05 level or better as determined by the chi-square test.

observant also. Conversely, where the group is non-observant, the adolescent tends to be non-observant as well. There is also a highly significant relationship between the attitudes of parents and children in this area — a finding which was anticipated in the previous chapter. It may be asked, therefore, whether the relationship between adolescent and peer group attitudes is not in the final analysis a function of parental influence, since parents sometimes determine their children's selection of friends. This question is examined in Table 8 in which parental attitude was controlled. It can be seen in this table that if parents tried to limit their children's associates to those who share the parental attitude they would be successful in only a little over half the cases. Furthermore, the relationship between the attitude of the adolescent and that of his peer group shown in Table 7 is not significantly altered. Whatever the attitude of the parent, traditional or non-traditional, the similarity between peer group and adolescent attitudes remains significant.

TABLE 8

Relationship of Peer Group Attitude to Adolescent's
Attitude When Parental Attitude is Controlled

Adolescent's Attitude	Observant Parents		Non-Observant Parents	
	Observant Peer Group PER CENT	*Non-Observant Peer Group* PER CENT	*Observant Peer Group* PER CENT	*Non-Observant Peer Group* PER CENT
Observant	83	38	75	12
Non-Observant	17	62	25	88
Total Cases	12	13	8	17

These relationships are statistically significant at the .05 level as determined by a combinational chi-square test using Yates correction factor.

There is, we note further in Table 8, a tendency for adolescents to agree more often with their peer group than with their parents: 22 per cent of the adolescents differed from their peer group, 36 per cent from their parents. Also it is apparent that membership in either the peer group or the family is not enough to explain entirely the adolescent's attitude toward this particular ritual practice. Had we chosen to predict the attitude of the adolescent from a knowledge of his family's traditionalism we would have been wrong in 36 per cent of the cases, as compared with 22 per cent of the cases using the peer group's position as a predictive device.

This is in line with an earlier warning about the hazards of employing membership in a single group to predict or explain an individual's attitude or behavior. The sharp increase in predictability which is possible when more than one group is used is readily apparent in Table 9. The data show that when both groups have the same attitude toward this practice, the probability increases greatly that the adolescent will share their attitude. Thus, in cases where the parent and peer group are both observant, 83 per cent of the adolescents say they will be observant; when both are non-observant, 88 per cent of the teenagers replied that they had no intention of using *kosher* meat when they married. The combined influence of the two groups, presumably both in terms of the examples they set and their expectations, was very effective: in all, only 14 per cent of the adolescents deviated from the position of these two groups when both held the same attitude.

TABLE 9

Relationship Between Adolescent's Attitude and Membership Groups' Attitudes When Membership Groups' Attitudes are Similar

Adolescent's Attitude	Parental and Peer Groups are Observant PER CENT	Parental and Peer Groups are Non-Observant PER CENT
Observant	83	12
Non-Observant	17	88
Total Cases	12	17

This relationship is statistically significant at the .001 level as determined by a chi-square test using Yates correction factor.

The Peer Group as Reference Group

Another more theoretically interesting way of considering the influence of the peer group upon the adolescent is to treat it as a reference group, not merely as a membership group. A membership group is a collectivity to which the individual objectively belongs; a reference group, on the other hand, is a group to which he psychologically relates himself, whether or not he belongs. Indeed, not infrequently a person will choose the norms of a group of which he is not a member in preference to those of a group to which he objectively belongs.

The following criteria were used to determine whether the peer group was one of the adolescent's reference groups: (1) perceived importance of the group to the adolescent, (2) whether the group was perceived as a model for self-evaluation, (3) perceived bond of understanding. The adolescents were asked these questions:

"1. Who are the people whose opinion of you is important to you?

2. How religious would you say you are? Are you comparing yourself with someone? If so, with whom are you comparing yourself?

3. Who do you think understands you better, your parents or your friends?"

The adolescent's responses to these questions enabled us to place him into one of three groups: (1) respondents who named their parents more often than their peer group; (2) those who named their peers more often than their parents; (3) those who named their parents and peers with equal frequency. The group named most frequently will be considered the adolescent's reference group, or the more important of the two groups — at least for this particular area. Of course, the adolescent may have other referents than those considered here: for example, teachers, siblings or other kinfolk; but for the present we shall limit ourselves to an analysis of peer and parental influences.

When peers and parents are treated as reference groups, the number of subjects who deviated from the norms of their group was very small. As can be seen in Table 10, no more than 14 per cent of the entire sample had an attitude toward the use of *kosher* meat different from that of their reference group. Equally interesting was the finding that while teenagers are more

TABLE 10

Relationship of Adolescent's Attitude and Attitude of His Reference Group

Adolescent's Reference Group	Adolescent's Attitude Is	
	Like His Reference Group (Cases)	Unlike His Reference Group (Cases)
Parents	21	5
Parents and Peers	5	1
Peers	15	1
Total Cases§	41	7

§ Two cases not included in which the adolescent described parents and peer group as reference groups but where the reference groups held conflicting attitudes.

likely to choose their parents as a reference group, they conformed more closely to the norm of their peers. Only seven per cent of the adolescents to whom the peer group was a reference group had opinions different from their peers. This finding was of particular significance in enabling us to understand the behavior of adolescents in situations where the expectations of parents and peers were in conflict.

Parent-Peer Group Cross-Pressures

The data so far has shown that adolescents perceived their parents and peers as important persons in their lives. Both groups exerted pressure upon the adolescent to conform to their expectations. Frequently these expectations were similar and mutually sustaining, but in some areas they were in conflict demanding of the teenager patterns of thought and behavior which were essentially incompatible. To what extent did this situation exist in religious matters? What was the role and influence of the peer group in a cross-pressure situation of this nature?

Various information lead us to believe that a number of boys and girls found themselves in a cross-pressure bind. An analysis of their membership groups revealed that 42 per cent of the adolescents belonged to family and peer groups with conflicting attitudes toward the use of *kosher* meat. Furthermore, these conflicting attitudes showed up in the *perceived* cross-pressures to which adolescents explicitly referred during the interviews. Thus, parental pressures and expectations were usually perceived as contributing to a positive orientation towards religion, particularly towards the observance of certain ritual practices. Adolescents often told us that they observed a particular traditional practice because of a habit formed at home, or out of deference to parental pressures and preferences. The peer group on the other hand was often held responsible (by adolescents and parents alike) for the teenager's deviation from the traditional norm. Respondents frequently ascribed their first transgression of the traditional code to the influence of their peers. Though this may have been rationalization, it was not implausible in the light of Yorktown adolescent activities.

Consider the case of one 17-year-old girl, a popular leader of the sorority: Strict observance of the dietary code was the rule at home. Her parents placed a high value upon the observance of the Sabbath and regular synagogue attendance. Until her entry into high school, she had accepted without much question the dictates of her family. However, when she entered high school certain religious proscriptions became irksome: she could not participate in school activities which took place on Friday evening; and eating on dates became a serious problem. After all, as she told us, "You get tired of eating cheese, and tuna sandwiches all the time."

Gradually she abandoned many orthodox practices; she began to eat non-*kosher* food outside of the home, rode on the Sabbath and was less regular in her attendance at religious services. At first her parents objected, but eventually capitulated. "They didn't want to make an issue out of it. You see, they know that all the other girls do it," she told us.

This is not to say that there were no instances in which peer group pressures were towards traditionalism and parental pressures away from traditionalism. Situations of this sort occurred, but they were infrequent and even less frequently perceived and reported by the adolescent. An example of just such a situation was the influence of two highly regarded girls, one 13 and the other 14 years of age, on their peer group. The two girls were traditionalists by Yorktown standards: they observed the dietary code, attended Friday evening religious services regularly and made a point of wearing a necklace with a Jewish star to public school. The other girls in the group regarded this behavior with something akin to awe; their admiration was possibly one factor which influenced the leaders to describe themselves as strongly religious; they were two of three adolescents in Yorktown who made such an estimate of their own religiosity.

Both girls were instrumental in changing the group's pattern of religious service attendance to a point where the girls were going to the synagogue more often than their parents. At first, the other girls went along because they would rather accompany their leaders than be alone on Friday nights. Eventually they established a pattern of fairly regular attendance. This group was in fact unique in its regular attendance at religious services. One of the girls told us,

> "I hardly ever went to services before I met them. I didn't see anything to it. At first, I just went along because C——— and M——— went, but now I go because I enjoy it, and I like to give the Rabbi a good impression."

The peer group, like the family, expected conformity to its norms. Some violation of the norm was permitted, but beyond a certain point deviation met with group disapproval, and the deviator, if sufficiently radical, was expelled from the group.

Several expulsions occurred during our stay in Yorktown. Typically, the target of peer group disapproval was a person who lacked enthusiasm for the usual interests of the group (dating, sports, etc.), or who was isolated from her Jewish peers because, as one of her former friends put it,

> "She isn't interested in the things we are. *She's very studious;* she doesn't go out much. She thinks we're not grown up enough for her, and we don't talk about the things that interest her."

Another girl, also under a cloud of group disapproval, was accused of dressing eccentrically:

> "G—— is a little queen. She wears high heels to school. None of the other girls would dream of doing it. She's always dressed up; she really dresses too old for her age."

Radical deviation from its *religious* norms will also evoke negative reactions and punitive responses from the group. We observed a situation of this type in the case of a girl, a high school senior, whose traditionalistic behavior was exceptional among Jewish adolescents of her age. She observed the dietary code, did not write, sew or ride on the Sabbath, and attended religious services regularly. She was commonly regarded by other adolescents as "fanatic" and "stiff necked." This attitude illustrates the ambivalence many adolescents felt toward traditionalism. They admired other teenagers whose behavior approximated the traditional norm, yet there was also hostility toward anyone who was too different or who would not participate in activities that the others enjoyed. Traditionalism was acceptable, even admired, up to a point, beyond which it became "fanaticism." The girl in this instance was quite aware that her relatively strict observance of certain traditional practices did not meet with the group's approval, for she told us,

"They make fun of you if you're really religious. If you don't eat shrimp you're considered a jerk."

The group had various ways — not all of them subtle — of expressing its disapproval of the deviant. Usually the malefactor was treated civilly, but coldly. He soon recognized that he was being snubbed. As the traditionalistic girl described above told us,

"When I come to the Center, they just ignore me. They stick together, and you feel left out. They all collect around the piano or something and don't ask you to join — you can't break in."

Ordinarily the peer group did not resort to a sanction so drastic as expulsion in order to bring about conformity to its norms. In most cases, the group achieved effective compliance by creating a climate of opinion which induced the adolescent to accept its norms willingly, often without his being aware of what was happening.

Between them, the peer group and the family appear to account for a large part of the religious pressures put upon the adolescent. The data suggest, as in Table 11, that when adolescents deviate from the religious norms of one group they are conforming to the norms of the other. Thus, of those adolescents who differed with their parents, 78 per cent agreed with their peer group. Conversely, of those who disagreed with their peers 63 per cent agreed with their parents. Here again we note that the norm of the peer group tended to be more powerful than that of the parents.

We cannot be *certain* that adolescents who deviated from the norm of one group were doing so at the instigation of the other. Adolescents may have rejected parental expectations because they disliked their parents rather than because they found the norm of the peer group more attractive. However, it is probable

TABLE 11

*Adolescent-Parental Attitude Similarity
as Compared with Adolescent-Peer Group
Attitude Similarity*

Adolescent and Peer Group Attitudes Are	Adolescent and Parental Attitudes Are	
	Similar (Cases)	Dissimilar (Cases)
Similar	25	14
Dissimilar	7	4
Total Cases	32	18

that the group with which the teenager agreed played a supportive, if not an active, role in alienating the adolescent from the norm of the other group. Few adolescents were in rebellion against both groups. Logically, the adolescent could have agreed with both groups, with one of the two or with none; yet in only 8 per cent of the cases did he take the last alternative. This seems to indicate a need for support from at least one of these two important groups.

We can now ask the question: When peers and parents have conflicting attitudes, with which group does the adolescent tend to agree? More specifically: When the position of the family and the peer group toward the use of *kosher* meat was different, with which group was the adolescent most likely to side? The answer is the peer group. The data in Table 12 show that in those cases where parents and peer group were in conflict on the issue, almost three quarters of the adolescents agreed with their peers, as compared with only about a quarter who sided with their parents. In each case the group with which he agreed was about four times as likely to be his reference group as was the group with which he did not agree.

TABLE 12

Relationship of Adolescent's Choice of Reference
Group to Adolescent-Membership Groups' Attitude
Similarity in Cases Where the Groups Differ

Adolescent's Reference Group	Adolescent's Attitude Is	
	Unlike Parents and Like Peer Group Per Cent	Unlike Peer Group and Like Parents Per Cent
Parents	21	80
Peers	79	20
Total Cases	14	5

This relationship is statistically significant at the .06 level as determined by a chi-square test using Yates correction factor.

The finding that adolescents turn more often to peers than to parents when caught in a conflict is in keeping with a growing body of theory and data which point to the increasing importance of the peer group in the socialization process. Riesman (1953) has offered an intriguing explanation of the growing influence of peers upon individuals in our society. He suggests that American character structure is changing: that the relative number of "other-directed" persons (those who take their direction primarily from peers) is growing while the proportion of "inner-directed" persons (those who are guided by parental norms internalized early in life) is declining. This theory provides a valuable guide to future research on the topic.

Whatever future research may reveal about the importance of the peer group in childhood and adulthood, it will possibly find that at no other time in life is the peer group as important to the individual as in adolescence. In our society, the lag between physiological and social maturity creates a host of problems for the adolescent. In his efforts to cope with these problems, he often turns to his peers for companionship, recognition and support. The peer group provides the adolescent with a sense of belonging at a time when conflicting loyalties, identifications and values make him unsure of himself. Within the peer group the adolescent is able to acquire the status often denied to him in the adult world — a status which is based upon values he understands and can fulfill.

Minority Group Influences and Pressures

The impact of two important primary groups — the family and the peer group — upon the adolescent have now been examined. We have seen how the religious attitudes and behavior of Jewish adolescents were affected by the expectations, attitudes and behavior of their parents and peers. But we know that adolescents are also members of *secondary* groups. Some of these groups are large, inclusive portions of the population, as in the case of ethnic, religious, regional or sectional groups. Others are much smaller, numbering perhaps several dozen persons, as in the case of recreational groups or high school classes in which contact is too impersonal to warrant the label "primary group."

How important are secondary groups in shaping the Jewish adolescent's religious attitudes and behavior? In what ways are their influences expressed? What pressures and demands do they place upon the Jewish adolescent insofar as religion is concerned? In the remaining chapters of this study, we shall examine data which offer some answers to these questions. Two important groups will be discussed — the ethnic group and the national society. We shall show how these two groups sometimes place the Jewish adolescent under conflicting pressures. We believe that the religious attitudes and behavior of many Jewish adolescents can in part be understood within the context of this cross-pressure situation.

In this chapter and the following one, we shall describe this cross-pressure situation in some detail, specifying minority group and society pressures and examining the areas in which they are in conflict.

THE CROSS-PRESSURE SITUATION

Despite differences in size and composition there is one thing that secondary groups have in common, insofar as they are groups possessing norms, values and goals: they seek to transmit and enforce their own norms and values. Every social group requires a certain amount of conformity to the rules, standards and values which mold and regulate the action of its members. Without a minimum conformity to group norms the centrifugal forces within the group would in time destroy it.

Since most people in a heterogeneous society belong to a number of secondary groups, it is possible that the individual may feel himself caught between the cross-pressures of the conflicting values systems and role assignments of his membership groups. Sherif (1948) put it this way:

"Many a person today necessarily moves in different groups which may and do exert different and contradictory demands on him. They tend to pull him in different directions, to give rise in him to different (and not infrequently contradictory) values, norms, loyalties, and conformities. They contribute their share to conflict situations with unfortunate consequences for him."[1]

This is precisely the uncomfortable position in which the Jewish adolescent may find himself. He is a member of two large groups, each possessing a set of norms which are not completely dissimilar, but nonetheless not wholly alike or always compatible. To some extent both groups differ in history, values, customs and practices. They have existed side by side for many years: sometimes in harmony, sometimes in discord; sometimes with much interaction, sometimes virtually isolated from each other.

One of these groups is the general society — the group encompassing almost everyone within its national boundaries. The general society is the largest social unit with legitimate power to command the allegiance and obedience of its members. Its norms take priority over those of any subgroup within its borders. The society-at-large has vast powers to shape the attitudes and behavior of its members. Through formal education and the mass media it transmits a basic culture which most of its members can share; it possesses cultural symbols with which nearly everyone can identify: the flag, the anthem, historical and popular heroes. When an individual deviates from the norms through hostile acts, political dissent or simple and silent lack of identification, society can with violent or subtle ruthlessness, enforce its demands.

The other group is smaller, less powerful, but nonetheless real. It is a sub-society that is part reality and part myth. It has no borders, no government, no police. There has never been a census taken of all its members; no one knows for certain who its members are, but its existence is tacitly recognized by most Jews and non-Jews. It has created the world of syna-

---

[1] Muzafer Sherif, *op. cit.*, p. 123.

gogues, temples, Jewish social clubs, Jewish centers, Jewish welfare drives and hot pastromi sandwiches. It is, in short, that sub-group called the American Jewish community — a state of mind, not a state of power.

The Jewish adolescent is a member of the minority group and the national society; both exert various pressures upon him. Ofttimes these pressures are mutually sustaining, driving toward the same goal; but in some areas, as in religion, they are in conflict, demanding from the adolescent patterns of thought and behavior that are incompatible. The minority group seeks to transmit to its young members certain beliefs and values, some of which are religious (religion being historically important in Jewish life) as a means of insuring group survival. On the other hand, the majority group exerts, not always consciously, influences and pressures which tend to alienate the Jewish adolescent from his ethnic group and its religion. These pressures and influences undermine his faith in certain religious beliefs and practices and create a climate of opinion which induces the Jew to question the validity of group separateness. Moreover, they weaken the educational apparatus whereby particularistic beliefs and values are transmitted to new generations.

Group pressures can be distinguished by their goals and the manner in which they are applied. The two basic goals of minority group pressures are to keep the adolescent within the group and to increase his religiosity, a stronger commitment to the group being considered a happy by-product of religious interest. Both pressures may, and frequently do, occur simultaneously in the same community.

Pressures may be applied informally or formally. By informal pressures we mean the individualistic or non-concerted efforts of the group to control its members by means of gossip, ridicule, praise and so forth. Formal pressures are the conscious efforts of the group, acting through institutional media, to promote its welfare and insure its survival.

In this chapter we propose to examine some formal and informal pressures which are placed on the adolescent by the *minority* group and are designed primarily to effect his religiosity. We shall describe how these pressures operate within one specific group — the Jewish community of Yorktown, New York. In order to adequately describe the nature of minority group pressures and the manner and effectiveness of their application, we must first examine briefly a few essential characteristics of the Jewish community. No effort will be made to present a detailed picture of the community, for little would be gained by adding to the already large number of descriptive studies of Jewish communities, many of them approximately the same size as Yorktown. (c.f., studies by Sklare and Vosk (1957), Kaplan (1957), and Gordon (1959).) Rather our aim will be to point up certain community attributes which, though not limited to Yorktown, are so intimately related to the functioning of minority pressures upon adolescents that they need emphasis.

SOME CHARACTERISTICS OF THE YORKTOWN JEWISH COMMUNITY

Size

The most important thing to understand about the Jewish community of Yorktown is that it is small. According to a census taken at the time of this study by the local Jewish Center, there were about 1200 Jews in Yorktown, constituting about 2 per cent of the town's total population.

With a population this small it was possible for every member of the community to meet most, if not all, of his fellow "ethnics." The group's small size also permitted a high degree of interaction between individuals so that many members of the community learned to know each other quite well.

The smallness of the community was a theme which repeatedly recurred in our conversations with adults and adolescents alike. Adults were likely to take comfort in the group's smallness: it offered an opportunity for an economic and social sense of security which was denied them in the large city. As a migrant from New York City put it:

> "I was lost in the Bronx. I was a little fish in a big sea. Here people take an interest in me. If you're willing to hustle you can go places in this town."

Adolescents took a far less sanguine view of the community's small size. Typical of their comments were the following:

> "Yorktown is a dull town; it's too small. There aren't enough Jewish kids. There are only three other Jewish girls my age; in some classes I'm the only Jew. There aren't enough boys to go around."

The teenagers had ample reason to complain. We have already noted that the size of the adolescent group was partly responsible for friction within the formal youth groups. It had also created a dating problem. Because of repeated interaction during childhood, Jewish adolescents became bored with one another. They recognized each other's faults, idiosyncrasies and mannerisms; they had gone to school together; they had fought together, played together and worked together: as adolescents they found little excitement in dating one another. As one boy said, they felt toward each other "like brothers and sisters."

Economic Status and Place of National Origin

The Jewish community in Yorktown was predominantly middle class. There were, of course, a few wealthy manufacturers, a small group of professionals, and an even smaller working class element — mostly skilled artisans and lower paid clerical workers. But in the main, Jews in Yorktown earned their livelihood in typical middle class occupations such as storekeeper, wholesaler, insurance agent, realtor, and other small entrepreneurial vocations.

This occupational distribution was reflected in the occupations of the parents of adolescents in the Yorktown sample. 60 per cent of the group came from families in which the father was a small business man, usually a retail merchant, or a high salaried white collar employee; 22 per cent were the children of professionals, executives, or manufacturers; and 18 per cent were minor clerical personnel or skilled artisans.

The vast majority of Yorktown's adult Jews were either immigrants or the children of immigrants — most of them from East Europe. Only a few could trace their ancestry back to the German peddlers who had settled in Yorktown a century before. This similarity in class and place of national origin was partly responsible for the style of life common to most Jews in Yorktown. In this respect the community was truly middle class. The manner in which leisure time was spent, the modes of dress, level of cultural attainment and social aspiration were typical of what is commonly attributed to the middle class, and was remarkably similar among the various occupational and income strata. Their common style of life facilitated interaction between the Jews of Yorktown and was, we believe, partly responsible for community's remarkable cohesiveness.

Organizations

Another important characteristic of the community was the pervasive influence of formal organizations in group life. Almost everyone belonged to at least one Jewish organization. The unaffiliated were pursued relentlessly and bombarded by innumerable appeals, until most capitulated. Any mention of Jewish organizations was likely to bring a wry smile to the lips of Yorktown's Jews. Leaning back in his chair one afternoon, an informant, one of the leaders of the Jewish community, remarked,

"Yorktown is over-organized. In this town everybody belongs to an organization. If you see a Jewish fellow walking
down the street you know he is a member of something, or
if he isn't he soon will be. If he doesn't join some organization there's something wrong with him. Nobody escapes."

Other data seem to bear this out. Only one adolescent in
the Yorktown group said that his parents were not members of
a Jewish organization. The Sisterhood, Ladies Auxiliary, Men's
Club, Zionist Organization, B'nai B'rith all vied for the time
and resources of Yorktown's Jews. Their activities gave the
community its appearance of integration and tightly-knit cohesiveness. It was through these organizations that the community satisfied the status striving and social proclivities of many
of its members, while carrying on activities to insure the welfare
and survival of the group.

GROUP PRESSURES AND ETHNIC SEPARATENESS: THE VILLAGE ETHOS

The smallness of the group, its essentially middle class style
of life which facilitated social interaction and the high degree
to which it was organized led some Yorktowners to compare
their community with a ghetto. It was hardly a ghetto, but it
could be compared to a village, and here the resemblance was
striking. For example, like an autonomous village, the Jewish
community had its own semi-official officers — mostly members of the Board of Directors of the Jewish Center, Welfare
Fund or B'nai B'rith. They were frequently "men with the
buck," "the big guys" whose financial status permitted them to
make large contributions to Jewish causes and organizations.
Because of their strategic positions in well known businesses,
they were often chosen as the community's representatives to
the gentile community.

The Jewish community also had its own supplementary school system: the synagogue-sponsored Hebrew School (*Cheder*) and the temple-operated Sunday School. To support these and other operations the community solicited contributions from its members. Large sums of money were raised to support Jewish activities in Yorktown, the nation and overseas. Many Jews regarded these contributions to the Jewish Center, United Jewish Appeal and other "drives" as legitimate *taxes* to support institutions for which everyone shared some moral responsibility — not merely as donations to charity.

Most significantly, the community exhibited a distinct village psychology. There was a feeling that one knew everyone, that one was known by everyone — *and was being watched by everyone.*

As in a village the individual felt himself surrounded by omnipresent observers who watched and appraised him, and who were ever eager to report his behavior to others. In one of our first interviews in Yorktown a young woman remarked,

> "Yorktown is too small. Everybody knows you and you know everybody else. You can't meet any new people. If you're lucky to go out with a new fellow, they come over to talk to you. They're not interested in you; they just want to look your date over."

The effect of the village ethos on the adolescent was especially pervasive. Each adolescent felt he was being watched, and that his private conduct — especially if any infraction of the group's norms was involved — would be speedily reported to his parents and friends. One 17-year-old boy told us a bit ruefully, "If you call up a girl Friday night, everybody knows about it by Saturday." In a similar vein a 16-year-old girl remarked:

> "This town is a web for gossip. One person says something and zoom — it's all over town. My brother was in a bar and

before he got home some Jewish lady called up to tell Mother he was drinking."

There were, however, pleasant aspects to the village ethos. Villagers are sometimes known for their willingness to help one another in times of crisis and for the pride they take in the group's achievements. Yorktown's Jewry boasted that it "takes care of its own." It generously aided its indigent elderly and all its unfortunates.

There was genuine satisfaction throughout the community when a member of the group achieved some distinction, particularly if a youngster was involved. The community took great interest in its youth. A considerable amount of money and energy was expended in providing recreational and educational facilities for adolescent and pre-adolescent children. Even so routine an event as the graduation of its children from high school was marked by a community-sponsored celebration. At the time of this study the 12 Jewish members of the graduating class were honored with a costly and elaborately catered reception.

The village ethos exerted continuous pressure upon the Jew to remain within the group. He was constantly being reminded that he was a Jew and shared with other Jews an interdependence of fate. The following extract taken from the field notes of the Cornell Study of Intergroup Relations provides a striking example of the manner in which the informal pressure toward maintenance of ethnic separateness operated:

"Once a year the Masons have a communion breakfast. Each member goes to his respective church for services, then they all gather at the hotel for breakfast. The first year that a certain member, a newcomer to town, attended, a small number of Jews were there; they sat scattered among the Gentiles and ate the ham and eggs provided. This member said that he felt a little funny about it, because he was Jewish among Gentiles (even though he eats bacon and ham at home). The following year, this man was in charge of the arrangements for the breakfast. He rounded up a sizable number of Jews from the temple and *shul*. They held joint services, then came to the breakfast as a group and ate the lox and eggs which had been ordered when the arrangements were made. They came as a separate, distinct group — Jews."

Adults pass this strong sense of ethnic identity on to their children. Jewish adolescents in Yorktown, regardless of the number of Gentile friends they had or how thoroughly they disassociated themselves from Jewish groups, were keenly aware that they were Jews and in some way, often inexplicable to them, different from Gentiles.

Intermarriage Taboo

Nothing so clearly illustrates the force and effectiveness of the group's pressure toward ethnic separateness upon York-town's Jews as their almost unanimous opposition to inter-marriage. On this issue all social categories in the community were agreed. Synagogue member or temple member, adult or adolescent, rich or poor — all accepted with little or no reservation the strong taboo against intermarriage.

One father aptly stated the point of view of many Jewish parents when he said:

"The basic worry of every parent is that their son will marry a *shiksa*. Some mothers live in constant dread of it. When two mothers with marriageable sons get together you can be sure sooner or later they'll talk about it. They don't worry so much about their daughters. I guess they're more sure of them."

Stories of parents whose lives were embittered by inter-marriage were legion. These stories were told and retold by worried parents who embellish each tale with a skill that was almost masochistic. Their attitude was so effectively implanted in the children that almost all Jewish adolescents accepted the intermarriage taboo. Even those teenagers who associated predominantly with Gentiles were no exception. Witness this remark by a 17-year-old boy, most of whose friends were Gentile:

> "Marriage is tough enough; you start out with two strikes against you if you marry a Gentile. Besides, it would hurt my mother if I didn't marry a Jewish girl."

Of all the adolescents, the girls were most effectively controlled by the ban on intermarriage. They accepted the community's definition of the situation and refused to date Gentiles. Said one girl:

> "We have our own lives. They know I won't date a Gentile boy, and I don't try to fix them up with a Jewish fellow."

The boys had more freedom in dating, primarily because their parents felt helpless to stop them, but they knew they were being watched by peers and adults who regard out-group dating as a betrayal of the group. Said one boy:

> "When you go out with non-Jewish kids the Jewish kids talk about it. They act different toward you, and you feel it. Some of the girls won't talk to you if you go out with a Gentile girl. *Everybody seems to think it's their business if you date Gentile girls.* One lady told my mother I spend more money on Gentile girls than on Jewish dates."

The Sorority's New Year's Eve Dance

A dramatic example of the manner in which group pressures operated to strengthen group separateness and to enforce the intermarriage taboo was the furor caused by the sorority's New Year's Eve dance.

It all began when the Jewish sorority invited the Gentile sororities to a tea. The tea was so successful that the Gentile girls suggested an inter-sorority dance be held at the Jewish Center on New Year's Eve under the auspices of the Jewish sorority. The proposal met with the delighted approval of the Jewish girls. Plans were made to hire a band and to decorate the auditorium.

When news of the proposed dance reached some Jewish adults there was an explosion of furious protests. The sorority's adult advisor described it to us this way:

> "Mothers kept calling me up objecting to the dance and demanding it be cancelled. One mother told me we were throwing the children to the wolves, and that we were encouraging what there was too much of already. Some mothers threatened to take their children out of the sorority. So rather than risk ruining the sorority, I told the girls they would have to call off the dance."

At first the girls were shocked, then angry, then frightened lest the Gentile sororities learn of the controversy. The matter was taken to the Center's Board of Directors, but it refused to intervene. Finally, a meeting was called and all interested parents were invited to attend. None of the protesting parents appeared. Said one member, "They were afraid to let their children know they opposed the dance." It was decided to let the girls go ahead with the dance.

Undoubtedly, the motives of parents involved in this incident were complex, but without question the fear of intermarriage was a strong factor. One protesting mother remarked, "When the community pushes it, it only makes it *kosher*. Why tempt them?"

The protesters were not organized; they operated informally and intermittently. They were not able to stop the dance, but in the final analysis they did not fail. It seemed highly unlikely that anyone would soon attempt to hold another inter-sorority dance at the Center.

FORMAL COMMUNITY INFLUENCES ON
ADOLESCENT RELIGIOSITY

Two institutions in Yorktown, supported and controlled by Jewish organizations, had as one of their manifest functions the socialization of the child into the group's values and norms, some of which were religious. These institutions were the Jewish Center and the religious school. The Jewish Center in Yorktown was a secular institution; its primary function was to provide recreational and social opportunities for youngsters and adults in a setting which would strengthen the individual's identification with the group. The religious by-products of the Center's activities were not as a rule intended or even recognized by many persons in the community. The religious school, on the other hand, was obviously designed to inculcate a religious viewpoint and encourage certain types of behavior defined by the community as religious. It was in the school that the rabbi, the community's institutionalized bearer of religious traditions, had his most meaningful and persistent contact with the Jewish child. We shall examine the impact of both of these institutions upon the adolescent's religiosity. Let us begin with the Jewish Center.

The Jewish Center

Among the newest of the institutions which serve the group in many communities throughout the United States is the Jewish Center. Patterned after the Young Men's Christian Association, the Center was formed to answer a need which in previous days had been satisfied by the synagogue. As we noted earlier, the synagogue was once an important place of public assembly as well as a house of worship. It was customary to hold festive affairs and to discuss problems of public interest in rooms which were part of the general synagogue building. Even today it is still the practice in many communities when constructing a synagogue to build an adjoining hall in which social affairs can be held.

As synagogue attendance decreased, less use was made of recreational facilities within the synagogue premises. Even for those persons whose ties with the synagogue remained close, the facilities of the synagogue were often inadequate, particularly for adolescents attracted to athletics. To answer this need and to attract Jews who had become estranged from religion but not from the group, many communities built recreational and organizational facilities of which the Jewish Center in Yorktown was a typical example.

Most recreational and organizational activities in the Yorktown Jewish community were held at the Center. The Center's attractions were two-fold: (1) It appealed to people who were hostile to or uncomfortable in religious environs, and (2) its non-denominational nature enabled members of synagogue and temple to mix in an atmosphere which was not explicitly partisan.

It was this latter characteristic which accounted for much of the Center's effectiveness as a cohesion-producing institution. Jews from all stations of life and of various shades of religious opinion were able to meet in the Center to discuss communal problems, whereas such meeting would have been difficult, perhaps impossible, in either the synagogue or temple. Through these meetings members of the community learned to know one another, and developed ties which heightened their sense of group solidarity.

One of the reasons Jewish adolescents knew all other adolescents in the Jewish group was because they had been brought together by the Center's teenage program. The manifest purpose of the program was to reinforce the adolescent's sense of ethnic identity through increasing his contact with other mem-

bers of the ethnic group. Several teenagers told us that they had
not met their Jewish peers from other neighborhoods until
brought together by the Center.

As a secular organization the Center had no program of
religious education. Even apart from religion, some critics
argued that the Center contributed very little to the "Jewish
content" of ethnic life in Yorktown. Indeed, few specifically
Jewish cultural activities found their way into the typical Center
program, despite the efforts of the Center's director to introduce
more items of Jewish culture into Center-sponsored activities.
His efforts met with resistance from members of the community,
some of whom preferred to keep the Center "non-religious,"
while others were simply bored or indifferent to "cultural"
programs.

As an example of this objection, witness the response of
adolescents to the following question,

> "I understand that the Jewish Center is planning a cultural
> program. Some people feel the emphasis should be on Jewish
> subjects, while other people feel the program should be on
> topics of general interest, mostly non-Jewish subjects. With
> whom would you most agree?"

Only 32 per cent thought the emphasis should be on Jewish
subjects, 49 per cent favored non-Jewish topics, while 19 per
cent wanted both Jewish and non-Jewish elements in the program in about equal proportion.

It is difficult to assess the influence of the Jewish Center upon
adolescent religiosity in Yorktown. In our conversations with
youngsters in Yorktown, the idea that any portion of their
religious orientation could be attributed to Center influence
never once occurred. Yet the Center itself was influenced by
religious values and traditions. It was closed on all Jewish
Holy Days; no activities took place on the Sabbath; and the
Center's kitchen observed scrupulously the dietary code, de-

spite the fact that many of its members were affiliated with the Reform temple, or, though synagogue members, non-traditionalists so far as the food practices were concerned. The effect of this, we believe, was to strengthen in the child's mind the association between ethnic identity and religion — or at least certain traditional practices. The significance of this association for the adolescent's religiosity will be examined in a later chapter.

THE RELIGIOUS SCHOOL

The intimate relation between religion and the ethnic group is clearly expressed in the principal non-familial institution employed by the group to transmit its culture to the young — the Jewish school. It is noteworthy that, with the exception of a few secularly-oriented schools such as those run by the Zionists or the Workman's Circle, the Jewish school in the United States tends to be a *religious* school.

Frequently the Jewish school is operated by synagogue or temple authorities and taught by the congregation's rabbi. Its curriculum is heavily weighted in favor of religious training: the sole function of many schools is to prepare the male student for his *Bar Mitzvah* — a ritual marking the boy's entrance into the adult religious community.

Let us turn now to a description of some aspects of the religious training of Jewish adolescents, with particular attention to its influence on their attitudes toward traditional religious beliefs and practices.

Type and Length of Religious Schooling

Almost every adolescent in this study had received some formal Jewish schooling; over 80 per cent of the respondents reported they had attended or were attending a religious school.

There was considerable variation in the type of institution

attended and length of attendance, however. In studies of this type, defining length of education always presents a difficult problem. Some studies have used the *number of years* an individual attended a religious school as the basic unit of measurement. This introduces a serious inaccuracy since it does not take into account the number of times a week the pupil attended classes. The result was that youngsters who attended a school twice a week for a year were included in the same category as those who went five times a week.

We attempted to overcome this difficulty by utilizing the product of the number of years and the number of times a week a pupil attended as a measure of amount of education. For example, a student who attended three times a week for four years would have twelve units. Because of the larger number of cases and the more detailed information on the level of knowledge, we shall concern ourselves for the moment only with the Philadelphia sample.

As can be seen in Table 13, Jewish parents appear to take the religious education of boys more seriously than of girls. Girls were less likely than boys to attend a religious school, and their training tended to be less intensive. Parents were also somewhat more apt to seek out a private teacher for their sons, while they tended to place their daughters in formal classrooms. Yet the girls reported more years of schooling than the boys.

This seemingly anomalous finding is probably due to the importance parents ascribe to the *Bar Mitzvah* ritual. Both parent and child tend to look upon *Bar Mitzvah* as a terminal goal which provides a convenient point at which to stop his education. Since there is normally a drop in motivation when a goal not seen as an intermediate step but as an end in itself is reached, the boy tends to lose interest in continued schooling, while his parents lack the motivation to pressure him. Lacking this goal psychology, the girl continues to study until other factors cause her to drop out. Thus, paradoxically, the *Bar*

TABLE 13

Type and Amount of Religious Education by Sex

Type of School	Boys PER CENT	Girls PER CENT
Private	10	3
Classroom	64	76
Both	17	3
None	6	13
No Answer	3	5
Length of Education	*Mean*	*Mean*
Number of Years	3.96	4.66
Times Per Week	3.44	2.73
Total Cases	271	242

Mitzvah is both an incentive for the boy to go to religious school and one of the factors which shortens his training.

The Information Test

The term "religious school" subsumes so diverse a collection of educational efforts as to almost defy description, to say nothing of classification. A youngster who reported that he received religious schooling may have attended a school with only one teacher and a curriculum consisting of a few passages from the *Torah,* learned by rote and without understanding, in preparation for the *Bar Mitzvah* ceremony. Or he may have attended a large school with many well-trained teachers and a complex curriculum of material on Jewish history, culture and Zionism, as well as on religion. The goals of the school, the content of its curriculum and the methods employed to teach the youngster vary with the ideological bent of the supporting group, the predilections of its teachers and the expectations of articulate and interested parents. The influence of the religious school is obviously no simple matter to determine and much was lost by grouping all schools together as the nature of our data required. Still, whatever its curriculum, all religious schools expose the child to some aspects of religion. They might reasonably be expected to have some influence, positive or negative, on his religious attitudes and behavior — or, at the very least, on his knowledge of Jewish history and culture.

We administered a revised version of Nardi's test, which consisted of 51 questions on major events in Jewish history, and the meaning of certain religious practices, customs and holidays. This test was then given to adolescents in the large Philadelphia sample.

The test performance of the average teenager was not impressive. For the test as a whole, the modal score was 27 questions correct out of 51. On the history portion of the test the modal score was 12 correct out of 30; for the cultural and religious section the modal score was 14 correct out of 21 questions. Had 70 per cent correct been a passing grade less than a quarter of the youngsters would have passed this test.

We were more interested in learning the degree to which the adolescent's level of knowledge whatever its inadequacies, was affected by religious training than in discovering how well informed he was. On this point the data are generally quite clear: on the average, the more education the adolescent had, the more informed he was about his group, its history, traditions and religion. The adolescents were divided into roughly two equal groups according to length and intensity of religious education and their test scores were then compared. Since the level of traditionalism in the home might be a factor in familiarizing the adolescent with certain religious beliefs and practices this factor was held constant. The data in Table 14 show that adolescents with high levels of religious education were more likely to have test scores above the mode than were respondents with less education. The increase was greater for adolescents from relatively traditionalistic homes. Apparently it was easier to transmit information about Jewish history and certain religious practices and customs to adolescents from families where the atmosphere was sympathetic to traditionalism than to youngsters who found no encouragement for their achievement at home.

TABLE 14

Relationship Between Amount of Religious Education and Test Score with Adolescent's Home Environment Controlled

Test Score	Home Environment			
	Traditionalist		Non-Traditionalist	
	Low Educ.	High Educ.	Low Educ.	High Educ.
	PER CENT		PER CENT	
Low	69	23	81	54
High	31	77	19	46
Total Cases§	34	68	183	133

§ First Philadelphia sample only. Not including adolescents without religious education or who left questions unanswered.

Differences between education levels *within* each environmental group are statistically significant at the .05 level or better as determined by a chi-square test.

The Influence of the School on Religious Attitudes and Behavior

One would expect religious attitudes and behavior to vary with the length and intensity of formal religious training. And this in fact is what the data show. The longer and more intense the amount of schooling the teenager had, the more likely he was to be traditionalistic in religious convictions and conduct. But as the data in Table 15 show the effectiveness of the school in molding the child's religiosity was influenced by the home environment. The school was more likely to affect the attitudes of the youngster, particularly towards traditional practices, when the home environment was traditionalistic, than when his parents were not observant.

Still, even when the child came from a non-traditional home the effect of religious schooling could be strong, sometimes to the surprise and annoyance of his parents. Consider the case of a non-traditionalistic family, which for a variety of reasons was

TABLE 15

*Relationship Between Amount of Religious
Education and Adolescent's Attitudes and Behavior
with Home Environment Controlled*

	Home Environment			
	Traditionalist		Non-Traditionalist	
	Low Educ.	High Educ.	Low Educ.	High Educ.
	PER CENT		PER CENT	
Adolescent's Attitude Toward Beliefs				
Traditionalistic	39	53	18	29
Non-Traditionalistic	61	47	82	71
Adolescent's Attitude Toward Practices				
Traditionalistic	42	62	22	27
Non-Traditionalistic	58	38	78	73
Adolescent's Behavior				
Traditionalistic	19	30	5	9
Non-Traditionalistic	81	70	95	91
Total Cases§	34	68	183	133

§ First Philadelphia sample only. Not including adolescents without religious education or who left questions unanswered.

affiliated with the synagogue. They had sent their son to the synagogue's religious school where he was exposed for the first time to traditional religious norms and practices. The boy accepted the traditional norms without reservation and tried to observe them at home. At first his parents were impressed by his religious enthusiasm, but as the orthodox practices of their progeny began to restrict parental freedom they became annoyed. Said the mother of this nine-year-old boy, whose unsuccessful attempts to introduce the traditional dietary code into a thoroughly non-traditional home had created a family crisis,

> "I was delighted when L—— liked *Cheder;* it made it so much easier to get him to go. We didn't have to coax him like other parents did their children. But when he began to be really *frum* (pious) we didn't know what to do. *Of course we were glad that he was religious,* but we never kept a *kosher* house, and I didn't intend to start one just to please him. I had a hard time explaining it to him, but eventually he got over it."

INFORMAL COMMUNITY PRESSURES ON THE ADOLESCENT

The community also exerted informal pressure on the teenager which tended to foster and reinforce positive attitudes towards religion. By informal pressures we mean the unorganized activities of individuals acting without the explicit sanction of the community. In order to understand the direction of these pressures and the mechanisms through which they were applied, it will be necessary to examine the religious climate of the community. This will enable us to appreciate how the expectations of some adults, acting as individuals, could influence adolescent religiosity.

The earliest Jews of Yorktown formed a religiously homogeneous group. Most of the settlers were German refugees from the anti-liberal and anti-semitic reaction which followed the collapse of the constitutional movement of 1848. They appeared in Yorktown about 1850, bringing with them a form of Reform Judaism which was then popular among certain urban Jewish groups in Germany. In 1863 they built the first temple in Yorktown, B'nai Israel.

During the 1880's an oppression more onerous and deadly than the German reaction was responsible for the appearance of another large group of immigrants in Yorktown. These were East European Jews who had fled the governmentally inspired *pogroms* and grinding poverty of Czarist Poland and Russia.

Unlike the German Jews, the new settlers had not been exposed to the full force of Western secularism and liberalism. They had been, for the most part, inhabitants of small Jewish communities (*shtetls*) where orthodoxy was deeply ingrained in the social system. Not finding the Reform mode of worship congenial, they organized a new congregation. In the beginning they met in various homes for services, but ultimately the congregation moved to its own building on Plum Street. This Reform-Orthodox division persisted among Yorktown's Jews, although the original relationship between denomination and place of national origin had disappeared. Most members of the Reform temple did not come from the original German group, but from the more recent East European wave.

An overwhelming proportion of Yorktown's Jews were affiliated with a house of worship. According to a census taken by the Jewish Center, 92 per cent of all Jews in Yorktown (see Table 16) reported membership in either the synagogue or temple. This high rate of membership seemed to be more a function of the community's intensely organized character than of a high level of religiosity. Attendance at religious services was not remarkable. Daily services were virtually unattended, and it was estimated by the Jewish Center Director that Sabbath services at the synagogue were attended on the average by 80 to 120 people; at the temple by 60 to 80 people. From what we observed both estimates seem high.

TABLE 16

Religious Affiliation by Age in Yorktown

	Total PER CENT	*65 and Over* PER CENT	*21–65* PER CENT	*Under 21* PER CENT
Synagogue	59	59	59	61
Temple	28	34	27	29
Both	5	2	5	3
Neither	8	5	9	7
Total Cases	1200	83	786	331

By far the largest proportion of Jews tended to limit their religious attendance to the High Holy Days (*Rosh Hashanah,* and *Yom Kippur*), or occasional visits in connection with the death of a member of the family.

Only a few Yorktown families were thoroughly traditional in their observance of the food laws. One informant estimated that perhaps no more than a dozen families consistently observed all the aspects of the dietary code both in and outside the home. One woman who belonged to this category was well aware that her orthodoxy was atypical. She told us, half annoyed, half boastful:

> "I'm a freak. People can't understand it. Some of my friends think I'm crazy."

This is not to say, however, that the general climate of opinion in the community, at least on the level of "heroic idealism," was anti-traditional. Quite the contrary; many Yorktowners expressed admiration for the traditional norms. Moreover, a number of families bought their meat in the kosher market, despite the obvious inconveniences involved in there being only one *kosher* butcher in town. We have already noted that half of the adolescents in Yorktown came from homes which used *kosher* meat, and 54 per cent used separate "meat and milk" utensils and dishes.

Thus, while it cannot be said that the hold and appeal of traditionalism in Yorktown was strong, neither was it negligible. Traditionalism, however, was more apparent in the *attitudes and expectations* of adults than in their actual behavior.

Community Religious Expectations

The relationship of parental expectations to the adolescent's religious attitudes and behavior has already been examined. We turn now to a consideration of the influence of the general adult community upon the teenager's religious convictions and conduct. Yorktown's adults held a variety of viewpoints on religion and displayed many types of religious and non-religious behavior. To speak of community religious expectations under these conditions is at best a hazardous undertaking. Notwithstanding this diversity it was possible to discern several expectations which characterized major segments of the community's population.

To begin with, adults from all groups said they wanted youngsters in the community to actively support religion, not merely to accept its worth. This viewpoint seemed to reflect a strong feeling that children who are religious "will turn out better; they're not as likely to get into trouble." It was much more difficult to discover what adults expected of youngsters so far as specific religious beliefs were concerned. Like the adolescent, the typical adult in Yorktown tended to think of religion in terms of practices and customs; religious beliefs were considered the domain of the theologian and scholar. Continued probing in this area elicited only the expectation, characteristic of every-one with whom we spoke, that youngsters "should believe in God."

Yorktown's adults were more articulate and less homogeneous in their evaluation of the importance of specific religious prac-tices. Synagogue members were likely to stress the importance of the dietary code, while temple and synagogue members alike thought attendance at religious services highly desirable. The position of the synagogue-affiliated group was well stated by one of its leaders who told us:

> "Theoretically parents want their children to be religious. They would like it; anybody would. They would like their children to go to *Cheder,* keep a *kosher* home and take a real interest in the synagogue. *That's what they would like;* what they expect is a hell of a lot different."

A temple member stated the position of her group in this fashion:

> "Some of the mothers are concerned by the lack of inter-est their children show in the temple. We would like them to come to Friday night services; the rabbi tries so hard to interest them. Heaven knows we don't expect them to be fanatic, but it would be nice if they took an interest in their religion."

These were the adults' religious expectations, as reported to the investigator. But how did the adolescent perceive the reli-gious expectations of adults in the Jewish community? To find an answer to this question we asked: "As far as religion is con-cerned, what do Jewish adults, not just your parents, expect of Jewish adolescents?" Their responses revealed that 20 per cent of the adolescents thought adult expectations were largely de-mands that the adolescent maintain a keen awareness of his ethnic identity and do nothing to jeopardize it. Said one boy in this group, "They want us to go with Jewish kids, or not marry a Gentile."

A larger group, 42 per cent, felt that the community's primary emphasis was upon attendance at religious services, especially during the High Holy Days. As one girl put it,

"They don't expect too much when you come down to it. They like you to observe certain customs like going to the synagogue on the holidays."

Only 18 per cent of the respondents thought adults expected them to observe *kashruth* or attend Friday night services; 12 per cent did not know what adults expected, and 8 per cent said adults expected nothing.

These were the expectations of adults acting as individuals *speaking only for themselves,* as seen by the adolescents. They were not high, nor was much informal pressure applied to see that they were met. In general, as one adult put it, "They hope by some miracle that the children will catch it (religion), but they don't pressure it."

But the expectations of some adults *acting as representatives of the group* were quite different. A few persons, acting informally and individually, assumed on their own initiative the role of guardians of the traditional code, and sought vigorously to support and strengthen traditionalism among Jews in the community. It was largely a result of their efforts that the official attitudes and expectations of the community inclined toward the traditional norm. As we have already noted, the Jewish Center maintained a *kosher* kitchen, despite the fact that many of its members were non-observant. The Center was closed during the Sabbath and no activities (even with philanthropic purposes) were held under Center auspices during this period. Many persons opposed any community-wide activity which violated the orthodox code (although many influential persons in the community were non-traditional) out of deference to the opinions of this "guardian group."

The effect of the "guardian group" upon the adolescent was vastly out of proportion to its actual size. The "guardians" constituted the omnipresent "they" — those feared and respected persons who were ever ready to note and disapprove an adolescent's violation of the traditional code. Their influence was primarily responsible for the fact that no Jewish youth group contemplated holding a social activity on Friday nights. Adolescents knew that any such violation of the traditional code would bring down upon their heads the furious protests of this small but outspoken group.

We can evaluate the influence of community expectations upon the adolescent by comparing his *perception* of the community's expectations with his actual behavior. The religious behavior in this case was attendance at religious services, a practice endorsed by all denominations in the community. We know from their reports that 60 per cent of the adolescents perceived adults in the community as expecting, at the very least, some attendance at religious services. To simplify the presentation of the data we called this level of expectation "high." The perceived expectations of the residual group which reported no adult religious expectations or believed the community's religious expectations were essentially only a commitment to ethnic identity we called "low." Adolescents who attended religious services "most Sabbaths" or "some Sabbaths and High Holy Days" were called "observant," while those who attended services only on the High Holy Days or less were labeled "non-observant."

As can be seen in Table 17, adolescents who perceived the community as having relatively high religious expectations were far more likely to attend religious services than those who perceived the adults in the community as having low religious expectations. Note that 63 per cent of the former group attended services on at least some Sabbaths while only 25 per cent of the latter group made this claim. The difficulty with these data is that it is not clear whether the adolescent's religious behavior was a function of his response to the community's expectations or whether he was projecting his own self-expectations and attitudes upon others in the community.

TABLE 17

*Relationship Between Perceived Community
Religious Expectations and the Adolescent's
Level of Religious Service Observance*

| Adolescent's Religious Service | Community Expectations | |
	High PER CENT	*Low* PER CENT
Observant	63	25
Non-Observant	37	75
Total Cases	30	20

This relationship is statistically significant at the .01 level or better as determined by the chi-square test.

Fortunately, other data existed which suggest that in the opinion of many youngsters community expectations do play a role in shaping adolescent religiosity. They had little doubt that the norms and expectations of the ethnic community were (or could be) a potent factor affecting their religious behavior. Witness the responses of Yorktown's teenagers to the following questions. Respondents were asked, "Suppose you moved to a community where most of the Jews were strongly religious, do you think you would be more religious?" Seventy per cent said yes; 30 per cent said no. And to the converse question, "Suppose you moved to a community where most of the Jews were even less religious than they are here, do you think you would be less religious?" Forty-two per cent of the youngsters said yes; 58 per cent said no.

When asked to explain their reason for changing, adolescents almost invariably referred to the influence of other persons in the community. Said one 15-year-old girl:

> "People would have a definite influence on me. If everybody was religious, I would be too. It would be natural. I'd like their good opinion. Everybody tries to win the good opinion, not the bad opinion, of people."

A 16-year-old boy thought his friends would be the influential factor:

> "You would have more religious friends, and you would go to *shul* with them. You would do the things they do. You would become more interested in religion."

Lest it appear that the adolescent's response to community expectations was automatic, it should be noted that some teenagers stated they would not change no matter what the community norms were. Moreover, the adolescent's level of religiosity clearly affected his estimation as to how he would behave in another community. Thus, we can see in Table 18 that respondents who were relatively observant (79 per cent), as indexed by attendance at religious services, were proportionately more likely to say they would be more religious in a strongly religious community than were respondents who were non-traditional (61 per cent).

Conversely, the data in Table 19 show that non-observant adolescents were more likely to say that they would become less religious in a non-religious community (54 per cent). Only 24 per cent of the observant respondents said they would be less religious in a non-religious community.

TABLE 18

Relationship Between the Adolescent's Level of Observance and His Estimation of How He Would Behave in a Strongly Religious Community

Would Be More Observant in a Strongly Religious Community	Adolescent's Behavior	
	Observant PER CENT	*Non-Observant* PER CENT
YES	79	61
NO	21	39
Total Cases	24	26

This relationship is statistically significant at the .02 level as determined by a chi-square test.

TABLE 19

Relationship Between the Adolescent's Level of Observance and His Estimation of How He Would Behave in a Non-Religious Community

Would Be Less Observant in a Non-Religious Community	Adolescent's Behavior	
	Observant PER CENT	*Non-Observant* PER CENT
YES	29	54
NO	71	46
Total Cases	24	26

This relationship is statistically significant at the .08 level as determined by a chi-square test.

The non-observant adolescent was much more likely to believe that he would be affected by the climate of opinion in the community. The data presented in Tables 18 and 19 show that more than half of the non-observant group reported they would modify their religiosity in the direction indicated by the expectations of the community, while the observant adolescent felt he would respond more readily to pressures towards religious observance than away from it. An appreciable number of observant and non-observant adolescents appeared willing to change in the direction of increased religiosity if an example was set for them by the community.

This finding suggests that parents and other adults in the Jewish community have tended to underestimate the effect of their expectations and example upon the adolescent. Perhaps the Jewish adolescent has been waiting for much more guidance from adults, many of whom fear that such efforts would be interpreted as unwarranted interference and pressure.

C h a p t e r   N i n e

Society-Wide Influences and Pressures

Sometimes opposing, sometimes supporting the efforts and goals of the minority group are certain pressures and influences of another group — the society-at-large. On first thought, it may seem somewhat incongruous to consider an aggregate numbering millions of persons as a group, but there can be no doubt that the general society has unmistakable group characteristics. Thus, most members of the general society possess a common identity ("I am an American"), share elements of a common culture and strive for at least one goal in common — group survival, though severe disagreement exists at times over the means to this end. In addition, the general society possesses other characteristics found in many groups, such as a division of labor and a hierarchical stratification of its members.

The general society is a world of powerful symbols and ubiquitous agents of control and socialization. Unless he attends a parochial school, the Jewish child receives his formal education in schools dominated by the norms and values of the general society. It is in this world that his parents earn their living and in which he will someday also compete for sustenance, prestige and power.

The purpose of this chapter is to examine the impact of some society-wide pressures upon the religious convictions and conduct of Jewish adolescents. We shall show how certain major value orientations in American culture place the traditionally-oriented Jewish adolescent in a painful cross-pressure situation in which he must choose between conforming to the norms of the general society or to those of his religion. Society-wide pressures tend to undermine the adolescent's faith in those beliefs and practices which visibly identify the Jew as a distinct group.

Since society-at-large is an amalgam of the numerous individuals and sub-groups within its borders, it may be said that America's Jews, as members of the general society, *contribute* to the society's values, as well as absorb certain values which weaken ethnic group solidarity and alienate Jewish youngsters from some traditional religious norms. This statement is correct as far as it goes, but it must be remembered that not all groups contribute equally to the development of a society's dominant value-orientations and norms. Many values in American culture were well established long before there were significant numbers of Jews in this country. For example, one of the dominant orientations with which we will be concerned, the strain towards uniformity and conformity, already was quite evident in colonial times. Moreover, societal needs are not always congruent with the goals of all subgroups within its boundaries. As a means of insuring national unity and survival, society may require conformity to norms which are repugnant to some of its members. This is perhaps most obvious in times of crises, such as wars when the nation may require its citizens to violate deeply held religious and ethical beliefs.

No attempt will be made to analyze the impact of every societal value on traditional Jewish practices and beliefs. Rather, for purposes of illustration, we propose to examine three major society-wide value-orientations, and the pressures associated with them, which affect the religious attitudes and behavior of Jewish adolescents. These value-orientations are: (1) uniformity and conformity, (2) secularization, and (3) equalitarianism.

UNIFORMITY AND CONFORMITY

It has become fashionable in liberal circles to espouse cultural pluralism, but we suspect that the goal of the state and a value-orientation of a majority of the people is cultural uniformity. This ideal, as Williams (1960) noted, is by no means new in America.

"Even as early as the 1830's De Tocqueville commented on the necessity of safeguards against a possible 'tyranny of the majority' in America and thought that public compulsion had already penetrated into private affairs in a censorious way not usual in the France of his day. Nearly a century later Siegfried, another and more critical Frenchman, visualized America as a land of vast uniformity in speech, manners, housing, dress, recreation, and politically expressed ideas. In 1948, Laski pointed to an 'amazing uniformity' of values, thought that 'business mores' had penetrated the culture, and tried to show that 'the American spirit required that the limits of uniformity be drawn with a certain tautness.' "[1]

A clear expression of the value American society places on uniformity can be found in the concept of the "melting pot." Implicit in this concept is the notion that the alien comes to

[1] Robin M. Williams, *American Society,* New York: Knopf, 1960, pp. 450–451.

these shores burdened with old world ideas, customs and mannerisms. Before he can become a full fledged, 100 per cent American, he must merge his culture with others in the melting pot of American society. In this process, old world idiosyncrasies are removed, and hopefully the immigrant is transformed into an American who values the things his fellow Americans do. The goal is to make him more acceptable to and comfortable in American society. The effect very often is to put him in a situation in which he is under enormous pressure to abandon his own value system and accept the values of his adopted society.

The impact of American culture upon the immigrant has long been of interest to social scientists (e.g., Thomas and Znaniecki, 1927). Some of the research in this area which deals specifically with the Jews dates back more than a generation (e.g., Wirth, 1928). The fact that work in this area is continuing (Kramer and Leventman, 1961; Glazer and Moynihan, 1963), seems to indicate that the melting pot process is not yet completed, even among second and third generation members of ethnic minorities. An important theme which runs through these studies concerns the pressure which society puts upon the immigrant (and the strains which these pressures produce) to abandon the mannerisms, habits and values of the ethnic group and adopt the culture of the general society.

Lest this be considered solely a "Jewish problem" or merely that of the immigrant, consider the study by Child (1943) of the pressure upon second generation Italians in a New England city to conform to an "American" pattern.

"(In school) rewards and punishments are administered by persons who are thoroughly American in background and whose behavior is thoroughly determined *by a deliberate policy of encouraging him to act like an American* . . . The achievement of the goal of rising in status in the community is dependent, in large part, upon the individual's acceptance by non-Italians. It is the general American community, or its representatives in small groups, that can offer the reward of an accepted rise in status . . . The second generation Italian cannot escape from being a member of American Society and from being constantly shown that he will be punished, or will not be rewarded, by his fellow Americans for behaving like an Italian." (Italics added).[2]

Similar pressures beset Negro children taught by whites who often cannot identify with their students, and tend to lack respect for, or even recognition of, a Negro culture. This pressure toward uniformity may force the ethnic group member to choose between the norms and values of the minority group and those of society-at-large. The resolution of this conflict is often a painful process; not infrequently it makes the individual guilt-ridden and bewildered.

Yet, despite the discomforts and anxieties it engenders among members of the minority group, the pressure toward uniformity has functional consequences for a heterogeneous society such as the United States. Commonly held uniform symbols and modes of behavior help make it possible for American society to survive despite many internal clashes of interest and values. In order to preserve its unity the modern heterogeneous state must develop culture patterns in which most of its members can participate, and require some minimal involvement in a shared core culture. Elements in this core culture are those relating to basic political values such as patriotism, or to a lesser extent some aspects of popular culture: sports, Hollywood and the heroes of the entertainment world.

Modern science has given the pressure toward uniformity tremendous impetus. Through the media of mass communica-

[2] Irving L. Child, *Italian or American? The Second Generation in Conflict,* New Haven: Yale University Press, 1943, pp. 58–59.

tion, movies, radio, television and periodicals, uniform modes of thought and behavior have become available to everyone. One needs only the price of a movie ticket, a daily newspaper or magazine to learn the correct thing to wear, to think, to do — with the result that more and more people are wearing, thinking and doing the same things.

Possibly in no other group is the pressure toward uniformity as strong as among adolescents. Investigators have long noted the tendency for adolescents to create sub-cultures with idiosyncratic argot, food habits and amusement patterns. An example of this phenomenon is the striking uniformity in dress which can be observed among teenagers, both boys and girls.

Even a casual visitor to a college campus cannot help but be struck by the similarity in the attire of students. During the day, for example, the girls wear what amounts to a uniform — the same sort of shoes, socks, skirts, sweaters, etc. — which is all the more remarkable since presumably college girls are financially able to afford diversity in costume. Hollingshead (1949) noted somewhat the same tendency toward uniformity in dress among teenage boys in Elmtown.

"*Most* boys wear "dress pants," white shirts, and ties, with jackets or suit coats; very few, however, wear hats. *Standard* headgear is a visored, cloth cap adorned with a dozen or more metal buttons, toys, and animal tails." (Italics added).[3]

Closely allied with the pressure toward uniformity is the value placed on conformity. For when uniform patterns of thought and behavior evolve, the tendency is for society-at-large to demand conformity to that pattern. The pressure toward conformity, of course, is not new; nor is it necessarily pernicious; nor is it limited to the Jewish adolescent. All societies, ancient and modern, exact a certain amount of conformity from their

[3] August B. Hollingshead, *Elmtown's Youth,* New York: Wiley, 1949, pp. 405–406.

members. If society is to persist, its members must conform to the laws of the land, pay their taxes, perform military service, and in general maintain certain modes of behavior, according to accepted conventions.

What especially distinguishes the modern nation-state from earlier societies is its increasing insistence that *all groups* conform to a *nation-wide* pattern. Societies before the Industrial Revolution also stressed conformity. Indeed, they were likely to demand it, frequently backing up their demand with force — witness the ruthless extirpation of such nonconforming groups as the Lollards in England and the Waldenses in southern France. But there was no demand for conformity to a nation-wide pattern applicable for *all* sub-groups. There was no nation-wide pattern. Each group, whether ethnic or socio-economic was expected to conform to its *own* pattern.

Earlier societies regarded group differences and separateness as natural and beneficial. In fact, it was not uncommon for the state to insist that the Jews within its borders conform to the norms of their own sub-community. On occasion severe punishment was meted out by the state to Jews who broke the laws of their group, even though the Jewish community was prepared to overlook the violation (Baron, 1942). The Jew's culture and apartness kept him inevitably an alien in Western Europe. But though he may have been feared or hated as a stranger, he was not asked to give up his way of life. Except for spasmodic efforts to convert the Jews *en masse* by persuasion as in Italy or by threat of expulsion as in Spain, there was no sustained effort to make the Jews conform to a national pattern.

Modern societies, while in general more tolerant of the Jew as a person, make it more difficult for him to maintain a meaningful separate ethnic identity. America is no exception. More than a generation ago the Lynds (1929) noted the pressure toward conformity in business practices, art and leisure time activities in Middletown. Robin Williams (1960) detected pressures toward conformity in morality and noted the tendency among Americans to legislate morality — a tendency which dates back to the "blue laws" of colonial times and is still evident in current attempts to censor films and books.

Foreign observers of the American scene are especially likely to detect and decry the pressures toward conformity which American society imposes upon its members. Their descriptions at times, as in Ortega y Gasset's *The Revolt of the Masses* (1950), make it appear that all group differences (and individual excellence) in America are being destroyed by leveling and sub-group obliterating influences — a conclusion which appears to us to be extreme, though possibly prophetic.

It must be emphasized that we are not suggesting that America is a monolithic state, peopled by identical automatons. America, it is clear, is composed of many sub-groups with their own sub-cultures. Notwithstanding the pressures toward conformity, the noncomformist is still to be found in our midst. Nonetheless, we believe that the overall pressures have been toward eliminating dissimilarities between groups and toward making it increasingly difficult for ethnic groups to maintain their own distinctive ways of living.

The experience of the Jew in the United States is a case in point. American culture had a dramatic impact upon the immigrant Jew, and the pressure upon him to adopt American culture was remarkably effective, in part because he wished to become an American. The Jew quickly took on the cultural coloration of the general society. Except among Jews in a few surviving Hasidic communities, the distinctive stigmata of Jewishness, as for example, earlocks, beard and certain habits of dress, swiftly disappeared. Within a generation, in speech, dress and many aspects of life-style the Jew became much like his Gentile peers in the class and region to which he belonged.

In the area of religion, however, the impact of American culture has been more complicated and the process of change more subtle. Changes have occurred, of course, and are continuing to do so as the Jew responds to society's expectation that he become more and more like his fellow Americans, but their effects are not always easy to observe. There are, however, several areas in which the impact of society-wide norms upon traditionalistically oriented Jews, particularly adolescents, is relatively apparent.

One area in which the impact of society-wide influences in perhaps most obvious, and at the same time excrutiatingly painful to the adolescent, is that associated with dating, amusements and sports. The Jewish adolescent, like most other teenagers in American society, enjoys dancing, parties and sports. He participates in school activities, cheers the team on at football rallies and plays basketball with his friends. Many of these activities occur on the Sabbath when traditional law requires cessation of many activities. The Jewish adolescent who wishes to observe the traditional practices of his religion and at the same time participate in certain activities finds himself in a painful conflict. School loyalty requires he attend, and at times participate in, Friday evening basketball games or Saturday afternoon football contests. To stay away would be a mark of extreme disloyalty to the school team. In Yorktown his absence would be noticed and resented. The disapproval of one's peers in matters as emotionally loaded as school loyalty is particularly difficult for the adolescent to endure. And yet he cannot participate in weekend school activities without breaking the Sabbath regulations of traditional Judaism. The end effect is a painful cross-pressure situation.

Not only when he participates in activities with non-Jews is the traditionalistic Jewish adolescent placed in a cross-pressure situation. Since many of his Jewish peers have adopted society-wide weekend patterns of amusement and recreation, the Jewish adolescent who seeks to observe a traditionalistic Sabbath is virtually isolated from his peers. He is unable to attend parties on Friday evening, ride in an automobile on Saturday and, most important to the boys, participate in Friday evening or Saturday afternoon sports.

The importance of sports to teenage boys was made clear by one of Yorktown's rabbis as he discussed what traditionalists in the community called "the basketball problem." Typically, Yorktown teenagers played in or attended basketball games on Friday nights. Adolescents who did not conform to this recreational pattern were likely to find themselves alone. Now it also happens that Jewish Sabbath services are held on Friday nights. Obviously the Jewish adolescent could not play basketball and attend services at the same time. He had to make a choice; usually he decided to join his friends, Jewish and Gentile, at the basketball games. The rabbis bemoaned the adolescents' lack of interest in religion, and made attempts to induce them to come to services. But the lure of basketball and the desire to be with the rest of the gang was too strong a handicap to overcome. Said one rabbi, more in sorrow than in anger:

> "When I came here I had high hopes for a Sabbath teenage program, but I found it was virtually impossible to get the boys to come; they were more interested in playing basketball. And without the boys, the girls lose interest."

SECULARIZATION AND RELIGION

It is not an exaggeration to say that modern societies and their cultures are predominantly secular. Such secularity is evidenced in the separation of church and state which applies to most Western societies. Where the church and state are not separate it is the state which is dominant. In Great Britain the sovereign is head of both church and state, but she subordinates herself to an organ of the state — the Parliament.

Also, many areas of authority and administration formerly within the province of the church have been taken over by the state. Marriage ceremonies, divorce decrees, hospital care, birth and death registration, and many other functions which were once in clerical hands are now performed, either in part or in whole, by the state. Most important of all, public education in most Western nations, Catholic and Protestant, is a state function, where once it was controlled and operated by the church. Many governments no longer concern themselves with providing religious instruction for the young. This is done by private agencies, either after public school on weekdays or on the Sabbath in Sunday Schools. Indeed the recent ruling by the Supreme Court regarding enforced praying in schools further emphasises the separation of church and state.

Students of the American scene are well aware of the strain toward secularization apparent not only in administrative or governmental functions but in general attitudes as well. Witness this statement from *American Society* (Williams, 1960).

"Much has been said about the secularizing tendencies in our culture. Although adequate research is badly needed on this matter the following observations seem well supported in a general way. It is variously noted that much of religion has become a matter of private ethical convictions; that the churches are active in secular affairs; that religious observances have been losing their supernatural or other-worldly character. It is said that religion in America tends to be religion at a very low temperature. Men of religious convictions note with concern the fraying of Christian (and Judaic) tradition as a new generation emerges having little training in, or attachment to, religious doctrine, and wonder if the 'moral capital' of the past is being dissipated."[4]

[4] Robin M. Williams, *op. cit.*, p. 346.

While secularization should not be exaggerated, the tendency in modern societies is for religion to be increasing separated from everyday affairs. Religion plays a smaller and more compartmentalized role in American life today than in the past; it tends to lie quiescent six days a week, coming to life on the seventh day — only part of which is set aside for religious observance. Human decisions and national policy today are purported to be based on reason and logic, or at least upon considerations other than the divine revelations and ritualistic auguries which inspired our ancestors (although, of course, appeals to God and religion are still frequently employed in support of governmental policy).

Religion versus Science

Nothing dramatizes the modern strain toward secularization so effectively as the recurrent and by no means gentlemanly feud between some proponents of science and some supporters of religion. Davis (1950) called it the "implacable conflict" between science and religion.

Most Western societies, irrespective of their political and even religious ideology, encourage science. They exploit it for the power and wealth it produces; they extol its virtues and devote an increasingly large proportion of the school curriculum to teaching its principles and applications. In time of crisis the modern state is more inclined to place its trust in science than in religion; although as we noted, the religious "resources" of the nation are also mobilized.

It was perhaps inevitable that science, which has placed in man's hands the power to end his species, should affect the beliefs which seek to explain his origins. Decades ago clergymen noted the corrosive effect of scientific rationalism on the religious faith of young people. This alienating influence of science is still strong despite the pleas of sophisticated theologians and scientists that science and religion are concerned with quite different areas of experience, and need not necessarily be in conflict. Hollingshead (1949) made the following observation about Elmtown's youth:

"Adolescents who seek an answer to religious questions which trouble them are faced with confusion and contradiction in other areas of the culture. In their formal contacts with the church, they are taught to pray to God for an answer to their prayers when faced by a personal problem. In their high school science courses they are taught cause and effect relationships. The clash of these two thought systems lies at the bottom of their religious worries."[5]

In the ghetto or *shtetl* the Jew had been relatively isolated from the influence of scientific rationalism. The Jewish school or *cheder,* the only kind most East European Jews attended, was primarily an institution for the transmittal of traditional religious learning and values; science played no role in the curriculum. Not until the Jew was permitted to move freely in the general society — as early as the eighteenth century in Western Europe, but not until the twentieth century in Eastern Europe — did he feel the full impact of scientific rationalism. This impact was especially strong in America where the virtues of modern science were daily extolled in the schools and the mass media.

That scientific rationalism should affect the religious outlook of Jewish adolescents, as it had young people of other faiths, was inevitable; we observed that the average adolescent in this study found it difficult to reconcile what his biology or physics teacher taught with what he read in the Bible.

Adolescent skepticism is readily apparent in the answers given to this statement by Philadelphia and Nebraska respondents: "Modern science has shown that many things in the Bible are not true." Over half the sample (59 per cent) agreed with this

5 August B. Hollingshead, *op. cit.,* p. 247.

statement, 34 per cent disagreed, while 7 per cent answered "don't know" or left the question unanswered.

In our intensive interviews with 49 Philadelphia adolescents this problem was examined more directly by stating the question this way: "Have your studies in science ever caused you to wonder whether some of the things in the Bible are true?" Almost half of the respondents (47 per cent) answered "yes," 41 per cent said "no," with 12 per cent answering "don't know" or giving no answer. While to a follow-up question, "Do you think science has shown that some of the things in the Bible could not be true?" fifty-two per cent said "yes," 41 per cent said "no," and 7 per cent "don't know." Somewhat similar results were obtained when the same question was asked of Yorktown adolescents: 68 per cent said "yes," 20 per cent said "no," 12 per cent "don't know."

Skepticism which results from exposure to scientific rationalism is, of course, not limited to an appraisal of the Bible's accuracy, but tends to be diffused through other areas of religious belief and practice. Consider the data in Table 20 in which the religious attitudes and behavior of Philadelphia-Nebraska adolescents are contrasted with their responses to the statement, "Modern science has shown that many things in the Bible are not true." Respondents who did not question the accuracy of the Bible on scientific grounds were consistently more traditionalistic in attitude and behavior than were adolescents who agreed with the above statement.

New Naturalistic Explanations

Another indication of the impact of secularization on traditional Judaism is the frequency with which *naturalistic* explanations are given for rules which previously were related more closely to the supernatural. This was most clearly seen in the tendency of many adolescents to ascribe modern hygienic purposes to certain orthodox practices. Ritual washing of the hands

TABLE 20

*Relationship Between Response to Statement:
"Modern Science Has Shown That Many Things in
the Bible are not True" and the Adolescent's
Religious Attitudes and Behavior*

	"Things in Bible Are Untrue"	
	Agree PER CENT	Disagree PER CENT
Adolescent's Attitude *Toward Beliefs*		
Traditionalistic	15	46
Non-Traditionalistic	85	54
Adolescent's Attitude *Toward Practices*		
Traditionalistic	13	49
Non-Traditionalistic	87	51
Adolescent's Behavior		
Traditionalistic	5	23
Non-Traditionalistic	95	77
Total Cases§	448	259

§ First Philadelphia and Nebraska samples only. Not including adolescents who left questions unanswered. These relationships are statistically significant at the .05 level or better as determined by a chi-square test.

before eating was explained as a recognition by Jewish seers (centuries before Pasteur) of the danger of infection from bacteria; the ban against pork stemmed, they said, from the dangers of trichinosis. Ritual slaughtering of cattle was described as a hygienic measure safeguarding the health of the Jew from sick livestock. Thus 42 per cent of the combined Philadelphia-Nebraska sample agreed with the statement, "The *main* reason

Jews are not allowed to eat pork is because it is frequently diseased." One 16-year-old noted, "Kosher means clean and cleanliness is for health. The food laws keep you healthy." A 17-year-old girl, explaining why she would observe *kashruth* said:

> "I know that *kosher* meat is clean. We were told that pork is not healthy because of a disease — I forget its name."

It could be argued, of course, that scientific rationalism can have a benign influence on the traditional outlook of Jewish adolescents in that it provides scientific support for conduct that had previously been legitimated only in theological terms: But it should be remembered that religious conduct supported for its naturalistic functions is subject to certain hazards from which religious behavior based on faith is exempt. Faith is directed toward reality that transcends nature; hence, practices based upon faith are beyond refutation by sensory reality. Religious practice based upon naturalistic explanations or functions, however, can be challenged by new scientific data. This is precisely what seems to have happened to the dietary laws. A number of adolescents who implicitly accepted the naturalistic approach argued that modern methods of sanitation and food inspection have made the dietary laws *unnecessary*. One 16-year-old boy remarked:

> "I am entirely against the *kosher* foods and dietary laws, as these laws were based upon facts millions of years ago — no refrigerators, etc. Dietary and food laws are completely without logical reason."

A 15-year-old girl stated:

> "Many years ago the pig was a dirty animal and Jews do not eat anything that is not clean. However, it is alright now as all meat is government-inspected."

What will be the reaction of adolescents who stress ceremonial observance *and* employ science as a rationale for ritual observance when they come to believe that the rituals are no longer scientifically justified. One type of reaction was readily apparent in Yorktown: the abandonment of the rituals. Indeed, one of the more common explanations teenagers gave when justifying their abandonment of some traditional practice was that they no longer found it scientifically valid. Other reactions were more extreme. Some adolescents abandoned both ritual and religion, since they viewed the two as being basically synonomous. This reaction was less common, but it tended to increase as time provided more opportunity for scientific rationalism to produce its effect. Thus, the data show that the drift away from religion was greatest among older adolescents: all of the respondents who described themselves as "not at all" religious were over sixteen years old. This older age group was also more likely than their junior peers to believe that science had shown "many things in the Bible are not true."

Ironically, the stress on ceremonial observance may have the unintended consequence of jeopardizing the adolescent's adherence to religion. The emphasis on ritual observance to the exclusion of religious beliefs and ethics represents a simplification which makes religious commitment vulnerable to naturalistic, rational attacks.

EQUALITARIANISM AND RELIGION

As Myrdal (1944) noted sometime ago, equalitarianism is part of the American Creed, a conclusion more recently supported by Lerner (1957). Americans are quite proud and at times even belligerent about their equality. Equality has several meanings: In one sense it refers to the similar intrinsic value of every man. About this aspect of equality, Williams (1960) wrote,

"At the level of explicit doctrine, intrinsic equality is widespread in American culture, both in the form of specifically religious conception (the equality of souls before God, the divine nature within every person, and so on), and in the more secularized formulations that attribute an irreducible quantum of value to every person: "a man's a man for a' that," "after all they are human beings," or the categorical imperative to "treat others as ends rather than means." At the level of overt interpersonal relations, adherence to a sense of intrinsic human value is discernible in "democratic manners."[6]

Combined with this emphasis on intrinsic human equality is a resentment of any claim to special status not earned (a factor which Gorer (1948) argued militates especially against the Jews.)

People who keep to themselves (Jews are accused of being clannish), who are different (traditionalistic Jews set themselves apart by their dress, their diet, etc) are sometimes suspected of considering themselves better than other people. That the Jewish traditionalist considers his group a Chosen People, strengthens others' suspicion and disapproval. These people take the concept of a Chosen People to mean that to be chosen is to be better or more deserving than others, despite statements repeatedly made by Jewish leaders, from the prophets to the present, that the election of the Jews does not involve special merit or privileges, only special, more onerous duties.

The Jew's assertion that he has a special mission has for over two thousand years aroused the ire of his neighbors: Jews have been called "stiff necked" and arrogant, a people steeped in "racial pride." Such accusations were common even in countries and in centuries which regarded group separateness as

[6] Robin M. Williams, *op. cit.*, p. 440.

God-ordained. How much more open to criticism is the Chosen People concept in a society which extols equalitarianism as one of its major values. Since equalitarianism is often equated with democracy, the belief that one's group is chosen (and by implication better than other groups) is open to the charge of being undemocratic. What word carries more opprobrium in a democracy than *undemocratic!*

That Jews themselves can be influenced by the emotional content of the word is evidenced by the response many adolescents made to the statement, "It is undemocratic for Jews to consider themselves a Chosen People." More than half (56 per cent) of the combined Philadelphia-Nebraska sample, answered, "agree."

Moreover, when the answers to this statement were cross-tabulated with the respondent's acceptance or rejection of the Chosen People concept, as in Table 21, it was found that adolescents who considered the concept undemocratic were far less likely to believe the Jews are a Chosen People than were teenagers who found nothing undemocratic in the idea. Only 18 per cent of the former group accepted the belief as compared with 72 per cent of the latter.

While a single cross-tabulation is far from conclusive proof, it does suggest that some Jewish adolescents were reluctant to accept a traditional particularistic belief because they did not wish to be thought of or to think of themselves as harboring illusions of "racial superiority." Like the non-Jew they felt the Chosen People concept possessed latent assertions of Jewish pre-eminence. Reasoning of this sort is quite explicit in a comment by a 14-year-old boy who rejected the concept because,

"All men are created equal. If the Jews feel they are a Chosen People it will bring about prejudices."

TABLE 21

Relationship Between Acceptance
of Chosen People Concept and Belief
that Concept is Undemocratic

| | Chosen People Concept Undemocratic | |
Chosen People Belief	Yes PER CENT	No PER CENT
Accepts	18	72
Does Not Accept	82	28
Total Cases§	245	261

§ First Philadelphia and Nebraska samples only. Not including adolescents who answered "don't know" or left questions unanswered. This relationship is statistically significant at the .01 level as determined by a chi-square test.

Said another boy, 17 years old:

"There is no superiority of races. The Jews are no more God's Chosen People than any other religious sect. We are all God's children."

A FURTHER NOTE ON SOCIETAL PRESSURES

We have sought to examine the impact of three societal values and the pressures they produce on the religious convictions and conduct of Jewish adolescents, particularly as they affect the adolescent's response to traditional norms. No picture of an overwhelming pressure for conformity was intended. The pressures analyzed in the preceding pages are generally subtle, not brutally coercive. Few people today would think of driving Jews to church and exhorting them to convert, as was occasionally done in the Roman ghetto.

The acculturative process will be entirely misunderstood if the attractiveness of American society to the Jew is overlooked. There is mass culture for the majority; the theatre, museums and universities for those interested in intellectual stimulation; a multitude of occupations for the ambitious, the glitter of "society" for the status seeker, and a host of other things denied the segregated Jew, but which are available to the Jew in modern society. Not that ghetto or *shtetl* life was the stagnant existence early Zionists pictured it to be (Kaufman, 1949). On the contrary, Jewish life in the *shtetl* was certainly more cohesive, perhaps warmer and more meaningful than it is today — but it was unquestionably less stimulating than the exciting secular world ushered in by the Enlightenment.

Moreover, it would be a mistake to believe that the general society always exerts a negative influence upon the adolescent's response to religion. On those points where Judaism and Christianity are in agreement, the general society may even bolster Judaism. For example, most organized groups in this country support the belief in God. Hence, it is not surprising that only 5 per cent of the youngsters in this study said they did not believe in God.

It should be remembered, also, that religion is generally considered in America a "good thing," if not for oneself, then for the other fellow. Since Jewish adolescents as Americans have absorbed other general values, it should be expected that this point of view would also be internalized. Thus, we found that 71 per cent of the combined Philadelphia-Nebraska sample agreed with the statement, "Religion is necessary in order to lead a good life," while 86 per cent of the Yorktown group said "yes" to the question, "Is religion important to you?"

Particularly interesting were the instances in which adolescents explained their adherence to certain traditional religious customs in terms of out-group expectations rather than minority group pressures. One 17-year-old girl whose friends were non-Jews stated that she ate *matzohs* (unleavened bread) during Passover because her friends had heard of the custom and expected her to observe it. Another girl, 15 years of age, confessed that her synagogue attendance was due to the influence of her best friend, a Catholic:

> "She would think it was funny if I didn't go to the synagogue; she's very strict herself, and I want her to like me."

This sort of motivation was, of course, not limited to adolescents. One Yorktown adult, a man active in community and synagogue affairs, attributed his initial participation in religious affairs to the expectations of a close non-Jewish associate. In order to keep the good opinion of this associate, whose image of the "good Jew" was a picture of a traditional Jew, he began to observe certain religious customs that he had discarded a decade before.

These examples do not invalidate the thesis that some society-wide pressures *in the main* tend to alienate the adolescent from various aspects of traditional Judaism. By undermining the religious beliefs that legitimate the group's election and function, they make it psychologically difficult for him to maintain his separateness; and by penalizing him socially and economically for following practices which run counter to general societal custom, they militate against the continued observance of traditional rituals which historically have been important in Jewish life. However, it must be kept in mind that membership in a group so pervasive as the general society cannot help but be a force in the religious life of the Jewish adolescent, and that this force is not entirely hostile to traditional beliefs and practices.

Ethnic Identity and Group Identification

In the preceding chapters we examined some pressures placed upon the Jewish adolescent by the general society and the ethnic group. In the area of religion these pressures were at times in conflict: their ends were mutually exclusive. The situation was such that if the adolescent chose between the alternatives proffered by these groups, he must reject the expectations of one membership group in order to satisfy those of the other. We believe that his choice would be in part determined by his identification with these groups and the more the adolescent identified with the minority group, the more likely he was to be traditionalistic in religious attitudes and behavior.

Our purpose in this chapter is to examine the religious attitudes and behavior of Jewish adolescents within the context of group identification in a cross-pressure situation. We shall also examine the role of religion in the acquisition and content of ethnic identity. But before this can be done, the sense in which the terms "identification" and "identity" will be used must be specified.

The concept of identification has acquired several somewhat conflicting meanings, in part because an individual may identify with another individual or with a group. In the past the term has been used differently, depending on whether the object of identification was an individual or a group. In order to avoid confusion over terminology, we shall examine briefly some of the meanings attributed to the concept, while at the same time making clear how the term will be used in this chapter. Let us begin by examining the concept of identification with another individual.

INDIVIDUAL IDENTIFICATION

We understand identification to be a process, a way of relating oneself to some object. Freud (1949) explained identification as a defence mechanism which molds the ego after the pattern of a love-object. As he described it, an individual who identifies with some other individual internalizes that person's expectations, norms, values and other attributes. He may emulate the voice, gestures and other characteristics of the object with whom he identifies.

Sometimes the emotional tie with the other is so strong that the individual appears to behave as though he thought he *were* the object of his identification. In so doing he is able to vicariously share the feelings and situations of the other. Anyone who has observed a youngster seated before a television set watching a cowboy picture will quickly recognize the part emulation plays in individual identification. Dressed in a cowboy suit and clutching a pistol, the child vicariously joins his hero in pursuit of the villain, shooting and shouting in unison with the man on the tube.

It is the mechanism of identification with the individual which explains, in part, the strong influence parents have upon youngsters, as shown in this study by the marked relationship between parental expectations and behavior and the religious attitudes and behavior of their children. For the parent is ordinarily the first object with whom the child identifies, and the emotional ties established at this time are often extremely strong and enduring. The nature and strength of this phenomenon is a function of the critical role which parents play in socialization, and of identification in early childhood.

Identification appears to grow out of the biologically determined helpless condition of the human child. For a prolonged period, the child is utterly dependent upon others, usually his parents, for the satisfaction of his basic needs — a fact which in time becomes apparent to him. This situation creates anxiety and an attitude of dependency which expresses itself in a desire to be near the object which provides for his needs and to do anything which might be demanded in return for protection and support. Ordinarily, the child receives the support he requires, and in time develops a need to give love to and receive love from the parent.

Inevitably, however, for a variety of reasons, situations arise in which the child's demands are not satisfied. The frustrations produced by this situation undermine the child's confidence in his environment and generate feelings of rage and hostility towards the parent. How the child will handle his hostility depends upon several factors, one of which is his concern over losing parental love. The anxiety over withdrawal of love may lead to a repression of hostility and the incorporation of parental expectations, norms and values as a means of insuring the affection and support upon which the child has come to feel dependent. This response to the fear of loss of love is called identification. And it is identification which strongly influences the degree to which the parent is effective in transmitting his expectations and values to the child (Rosen, 1964, 1964b).

GROUP IDENTIFICATION

The individual may also identify with a group. We can discern two types of group identification — one of which we will call *categorical,* the other *referential.*

Categorical Identification

Identification is sometimes understood to mean the classification of oneself and others within a certain social category. It is a process of self-labeling (i.e., "I am one of them"; "They are like me.")

Categorical identification has two distinctive characteristics: the individual always believes himself to be a member of the group with which he identifies; and the individual does not necessarily have any affective orientation toward the group.

Essentially, categorical identification is an abstractive process. The size and kind of social category with which the individual identifies will vary as he proceeds up or down the "abstraction ladder." Thus, one may identify with all living things (e.g., the devout Jain who wears gauze over his mouth for fear of destroying life by swallowing a gnat), with members of one's sex (e.g., the feminist campaigning for woman's suffrage), with all members of one's nation, state, city or neighborhood, and so forth. In short, categorical identification is limited only by the ability of the individual to conceptualize his group memberships.

The individual who categorically identifies with a group may feel a strong emotional tie with other members of the group, but this is not inevitable. The Baptist, New Yorker or high school student may readily recognize his membership in these social groups but have no feeling for other Baptists, New

Yorkers or high school students, nor in any instance ever refer his conduct to the expectations of those groups.

Referential Identification

At other times, identification is conceived of as a process of reference group selection. That is to say, in referential identification the individual psychologically relates himself to a group so that he shares its values as his own personal motives; he adopts the group's definition of the situation, and in cases of strong identification will reduce his range of friends to those who share the group's norms. *It is in this sense that the concept of identification will be used in this chapter.*

Unlike the situation in categorical identification, the individual need not regard himself as a member of the group with which he identifies referentially. Indeed, in many cases the individual may identify with groups in which he is not a member but to which he would like to belong, e.g., the "bucking" private who takes on the ideology of the officer or noncommissioned officer social strata to which he aspires.

In identification of this type it is necessary, however, that the individual have an emotional orientation toward the group. When the emotional ties are friendly the identification is called *positive*. This appears to be what the Roses (1948) had in mind when they wrote,

> "We use the term group identification in its positive sense. It involves not only a recognition that one is a member of a racial or religious group because of one's ancestry, nor only a recognition that the majority group defines one as belonging to a racial or religious group. It also involves a positive desire to identify oneself as a member of the group, and a feeling of pleasure when one does so identify himself."[1]

[1] Arnold Rose and Caroline Rose, *America Divided*, New York: Knopf, 1948, p. 178.

Obviously some ways of defining and employing identification are distinct and others are not. One takes on the mannerisms of groups by emulating individuals belonging to those groups. Frequently the group with which one classifies oneself is also the group from which one obtains one's values. In cases such as these, there is little to be gained by distinguishing, say, between categorical and referential identification. But unless such distinctions are made in other cases, the individual can be said to identify and not to identify with the same group at the same time. That is to say, it should be clearly recognized that identification which is categorical (self labeling) is not a motivating force if it is devoid of emotional content, as it frequently is. We cannot assume that the recognition by a Jew of his membership in an ethnic group (categorical identification), necessarily makes that group's norms a frame of reference for his conduct (referential identification), just as it must be remembered that referential identification can be directed toward groups to which one does not necessarily belong.

GROUP IDENTITY AND RELIGION

We understand group identity to be a function of categorical identification. For if categorical identification is the *recognition* of one's membership in a group, group identity is the *product* of that recognition. Ethnic identity is a specific group label the individual applies to himself — not necessarily a label applied to him by others; although, of course, self-labeling is sometimes the function of the labels others apply to us.

We are probing for an individual's identity when we ask the question: "Who are you?" The response is often a list of groups to which he belongs. Thus when Yorktowns' adolescents were asked: "Who are you?" every respondent (after giving his or her name) located himself in several groups or social categories (e.g., "I am a boy"; "I am a Jew"; "I am a high school student," etc.)

Since identity is a function of categorical identification, the individual may be said to have as many group identities as there are groups to which he belongs. Which of these many identities will be salient at any particular moment will depend upon the social structure in which he is acting at the time and the affective ties he has with the group. Some groups, as we have already noted, are incidental to the individual. Towards groups of this type the individual has little or no feeling. Others are so salient that they intrude into social situations in which they are inappropriate. This was the case, for example, with a prominent Yorktown business man who told us, "I never forget I'm a Jew." His ethnic identity was an important factor in every social situation in which he found himself, particularly when the other participants were non-Jewish.

Religion and the Recognition of Ethnic Identity

Having clarified, it is hoped, the manner in which the "identity" and "identification" will be used in this study, we may now turn to an examination of the relationship between religion and ethnic identity. We shall raise and attempt to answer these questions: "What role does religion play in the process through which the Jewish child becomes aware of his ethnic identity? How does religion affect the content and meaning of ethnic identity?"

Unfortunately, little is known about the factors involved in a child's recognition of his ethnic identity, since few investigations of social development in children have dealt with this problem. Hartley's (1948) study of the age at which children become conscious of their ethnic identity is exceptional in this respect. He asked 86 New York City children, three and a half to ten and a half years old, "What are you?" More than half

of the children between three and a half and four and a half
years of age answered with their name; none of the older
children gave this answer. Very few of the younger children
categorized themselves with some ethnic group (Jewish, Negro,
Catholic, Italian). However, beginning at about the fifth year
ethnic designations increased in frequency up through the age
of eight.

Although an awareness of one's ethnic identity usually begins in the home, these findings suggest that interaction with
peers is also important. It is at about the fifth year that the
child begins to spend an increasing proportion of his time with
his peers, either at play or at school. Children often first become aware of their minority group membership when it is
pointed out to them by friends outside of this group.

Religion was the factor which first differentiated many a
Jewish child from his non-ethnic peers in Yorktown. Often, it
was because of some religious custom or observance that his
friends learned that he was different. This, at any rate, was
the opinion expressed by many Yorktown adolescents. When
asked, "How did people learn you were Jewish?" about two-
thirds mentioned a religious practice which had distinguished
them from their non-Jewish friends. For example, one boy
answered,

> "When I didn't go to school on *Yom Kippur,* they asked
> me why I didn't come to school, and I told them I was
> Jewish."

A girl, more traditionalistic than the boy, said,

> "During Passover I brought *matzoh* sandwiches to school.
> They all wanted to know what it was, so I explained it to
> them — I guess that's how it happened."

Other teenagers stated that it was their non-observance of a
Christian holiday, particularly Christmas, which first caused

their non-Jewish friends to question and recognize their ethnic group affiliation.

Religion and Meaning of Jewish Identity

Hartley observed that although most of the older Jewish children (8 – 10 years) in his sample were aware of their ethnic identity, many were confused as to its meaning.

Newcomb (1950) comments on this study,

"Even the oldest ones . . . had only vague ideas as to the meaning of the label. Most of them replied to the question, 'What does it mean to be Jewish?' by mentioning activities, like "talking Jewish," "going to the synagogue," or "not eating bacon." Most of them, moreover, like most of the non-Jewish children, showed a good deal of confusion in their ethnic frames of reference. To children it appeared possible to be simultaneously Jewish and Catholic, Catholic and Protestant, or American and German, but impossible to be Jewish and American, Negro and Protestant, or Catholic and French. Judging from these data, nationality and religious roles are not distinct for most American children of 10 years or younger."[2]

Apparently, Jewish children in Yorktown learn to conceive of themselves as possessing several group memberships in preadolescence, for none of the adolescents found any difficulty in understanding that they could be Jewish and American at the same time. In fact, both identities figured significantly in their description of themselves. Respondents were handed a card listing thirteen possible items (see Table 22) which might describe them. They were asked, "If someone asked you to describe yourself, which two items would you select? List them

[2] Theodore M. Newcomb, *Social Psychology,* New York: Dryden, 1950, pp. 521–522.

in order of their importance to you. Which next two would you select?"

About half of the adolescents selected being a Jew and an American in their first two choices; both identities were included by 75 per cent of the group among their four choices.

However, the vagueness and confusion as to the *meaning* of Jewish identity which Hartley discerned in young Jewish children was also present to some extent among Yorktown's adolescents. We found that many adolescents were uncertain as to what role religion played in determining their ethnic identity. Much of this uncertainty it turned out, was a result of an in-

TABLE 22

Responses to the Question: "If Someone
Asked You to Describe Yourself,
Which Items Would You Select?"

	First Two Choices	Second Two Choices	Total in Four Choices
Fraternity Member	1	4	5
Sorority Member	2	8	10
Teenager	16	14	30
American	25	13	38
Yorktowner	6	13	19
Academy High-school Student	8	10	18
South Side High-school Student	6	4	10
Boy	2	9	11
Girl	9	7	16
Jewish	23	16	39
South Sider	2	—	2
West Sider	—	1	1
East Sider	—	—	—

ability to decide whether ethnic identity was achieved or ascribed.

At first this seemed to be no problem at all. Thus in answer to the question, "What is it that makes a person a Jew," 42 per cent referred to religious behavior or belief, 46 per cent felt that a person was a Jew by virtue of his being born of Jewish parents, 10 per cent held a combination of both views, while one person (two per cent) was unable to give an answer. Adolescents who felt that being a Jew was a function of birth were explicitly defining ethnic identity as *ascribed* group membership about which one had no say. As one 17-year-old boy told us:

> "First of all we are born a Jew. It's part of heredity. We get it from our ancestors."

Adolescents who emphasized religious behavior as the essential and distinguishing element in ethnic identity were in effect defining identity as *achieved* membership in a group. As one boy carefully pointed out:

> "A person is a Jew because you believe in Jewish ideals; it's the way you observe the things you do, like going to the synagogue. You're a good *religious* person."

Still, on further inspection we found that not all of the adolescents who defined ethnic identity in terms of ascribed group membership were certain that birth into the group was a necessary and sufficient criterion for ethnic identity; nor were all the adolescents who defined identity as a product of religious behavior always satisfied that this was the essential element in determining ethnic identity. For example, in answer to the question,

> "Suppose a person is born of Jewish parents but does not believe in any religion: Would he still be a Jew?"

78 per cent said "yes," 22 per cent answered "no."

Obviously a number of adolescents who had previously defined ethnic identity in terms of religious behavior and belief
had changed the criterion employed in their definition. This
can be seen more clearly in the cross-tabulation of answers to
the question just cited with the answers to the question, "What
makes a person a Jew?"

As the data in Table 23 show, many of the respondents who
had defined identity in terms of religious behavior and belief
continued to consider a person born of Jewish parents a Jew
even though he had no religion: 67 per cent of these respondents
had changed their definition of ethnic identity from achieved
group membership resulting from religious behavior to ascribed group membership resulting from an accident of birth.
On the other hand, most of the adolescents who had originally
defined ethnic identity in terms of ascribed group membership
continued to regard the non-religious person born of Jewish
parents as a Jew. However, even in this group, 17 per cent felt
that ethnic identity would be lost if the individual had no
religion.

TABLE 23

*Relationship Between Responses to Question:
"What Makes a Person a Jew?" and "Is a Person
Born of Jewish Parents a Jew if He Has no
Religion?"*

"Is a Person a Jew Without Religion?"	Being a Jew is a Result of:	
	Birth PER CENT	Religion PER CENT
YES	83	67
NO	17	33
Total Cases§	23	21

§ Not including one "no answer" and five adolescents who believed
ethnic identity was a product of both religiosity and birth.

The same picture appeared when we cross-tabulated the answers to the questions, "What makes a person a Jew?" and "If a Jew converts to Christianity would he still be a Jew?" (54 per cent said "yes" to the latter question 44 per cent said "no," and 2 per cent were unable to answer the question.)

As can be seen in Table 24, more than a third of the adolescents who originally had defined ethnic identity as a function of birth into the group felt that this identity would be lost when another religion was adopted. Even more difficult to understand are those respondents who, though they defined ethnicity in terms of religious behavior nonetheless believed that a Jew would not lose his ethnic identity if he adopted Christianity.

TABLE 24

Relationship Between Responses to Questions:
"What Makes a Person a Jew?" and "Is He a Jew If
He Converts to Christianity?"

"Is a Person A Jew If He Converts To Christianity?"	Being a Jew is a Result Of:	
	Birth PER CENT	*Religion* PER CENT
YES	59	43
NO	41	57
Total Cases§	22	21

§ Not including two cases "don't know" or "no answer" and five adolescents who believed ethnic identity was a product of both religion and birth.

Much of this uncertainty as to what determines ethnic identity may probably be attributed to the assimilative and secularistic processes, characteristic of Jewish life since the Emancipation, which have blurred the social and religious elements that once clearly distinguished Jew from non-Jew. Many Jewish adolescents in Yorktown were agreed that "Jewishness" — the way one lives as a Jew — must involve religion, but in a world characterized by rising secularism and in a community where some persons were passively or actively non-religious and yet unquestionably identified as Jews, it was difficult to be certain that religion was a necessary or sufficient criterion for ethnic identity.

The problem of clearly defining ethnic identity is not a new one. Centuries ago Jewish leaders wrestled with the task of determining the criteria for ethnic group membership. Living as they did in semi-autonomous communities with distinctive legal rights and obligations, it was imperative for them to know who was a Jew and who was not. As a result of their deliberations on this score Jewish law is fairly explicit: a Jew is a member of a group. He can become a member in two ways: *birth* (being born the child of a Jewish mother) and *conversion*. As a Jew, he enters the covenant of Israel with God. This covenant remains in force regardless of one's behavior; he may be thoroughly non-observant, may even reject the practices of the group, without losing his membership in the group.

Some people have even maintained that a Jew may convert to another religion and still retain his Jewish identity. There is considerable historical basis for this reasoning. In cases where group membership is attributive and the out-group is hostile, group identity persists regardless of its content. History provides several examples of Jews adopting Christianity *en masse,* only to learn that they retained their old identity despite its new content — they had become Christian-Jews.

Hence, adolescents who consistently defined ethnic identity as membership in a group were in agreement with theological, legal, and historical precedent. Still, their reasoning often had a somewhat racialist cast. We were frequently told that ethnic identity could not be discarded because, as one boy put it, it was "in the blood." Another example of this type of thinking was the comment made by a 14-year-old boy whose mother had been a Gentile and whose father was Jewish; he was being brought up as a Jew:

> "When you're born Jewish it's in your blood. A person can't stop being Jewish just because he wants to. No matter what he would do, he would always be Jewish down deep in his heart."

Ethnic Identity and Adolescent Religiosity

Were teenagers who defined ethnic identity primarily in religious terms more traditionalistic than those who stressed biological inheritance as the principal criterion of ethnic identity? The answer to this question would not be easy to predict if religion were defined in moral-ethical terms. Among Yorktown's Jews there is not necessarily a relationship between traditionalism and ethical or moral philosophy. It will be remembered, however, that the vast majority of the adolescents in this study defined religiosity in terms of traditional practices and observance. Hence, one might reasonably expect that adolescents who defined ethnic identity in religious terms would be more traditionalistic than those who gave a definition based on birth. Indeed, this is what an analysis of the data revealed.

Thus, when the criterion employed in defining ethnic identity was cross-tabulated (see Table 25) with the adolescent's level of traditionalism, as described in Chapter 5, we found that adolescents who defined ethnic identity in terms of religious practice and belief were significantly more traditionalistic than those who saw ethnic identity as primarily an inherited status. Unfortunately, it is not possible to know from these data whether this relationship is causal. Nor can we be sure, assuming that there is a causal nexus, which variable is the cause and which the effect. Quite probably the relationship between identity and religiosity is affected by the adolescent's commitment to his identity, as reflected in his identification with the minority group, and his perception of the role religion plays in group survival. We turn now to an examination of this problem.

TABLE 25

Relationship Between Criterion Used
in Defining Ethnic Identity and the Adolescent's
Religious Attitudes and Behavior

	Being a Jew is a Result of	
	Birth PER CENT	Religion PER CENT
Adolescent's Attitude Toward Beliefs		
Traditionalistic	22	45
Non-Traditionalistic	78	55
Adolescent's Attitude Toward Practices		
Traditionalistic	17	62
Non-Traditionalistic	83	38
Adolescent's Behavior		
Traditionalistic	13	38
Non-Traditionalistic	87	62
Total Cases§	23	21

§ Not including one "no answer" and five adolescents who believed that ethnic identity was a product of both birth and religion.

These relationships are statistically significant at the .05 level or better as determined by the chi-square test using Yates correction factor.

GROUP IDENTIFICATION AND ADOLESCENT RELIGIOSITY

As we have seen, Jewish adolescents in American society are sometimes confronted by a cross-pressure situation produced by the conflicting expectations and pressures of the minority group and the general society. In the area of religion, the adolescent, particularly if he is a traditionalist, may be required to choose between observing the traditions of the minority group or the norms of the general society — although the latter may be mediated through the expectations of non-traditionalistic Jews as well as by members of the society at large. What his choice will be depends, in part, upon the degree to which the adolescent identifies with the minority group. We believe that the stronger the adolescent's identification with the minority group, the more likely it is that he would be a traditionalist.

It will be remembered that we were concerned with *referential* identification, defined as a positive orientation toward the group, not merely a recognition of one's membership in that group. Group identifications are not mutually exclusive. The adolescent may identify categorically and referentially with both the general society and the ethnic groups. Indeed considering the important role these groups play in their lives, it is highly likely that most Jewish adolescents identify to some degree with both. However, we think it probable that the adolescent will identify more with one group than with another, and it is in these terms that the relationship between identification and religiosity will be considered.

Our first task was to obtain a measure of ethnic group identification — no easy task. We shall begin our analysis of the relationship between identification and religiosity by examining the index of identification used in this study.

The Identification Index

The concept of Jewish group identification is multi-dimensional, as both Lazerwitz (1953) and Geismar (1954) have noted in their research. Lazerwitz identified seven "criteria" and Geismar eight "categories" which they felt indicated areas in which the Jew could identify with his ethnic group. Our analysis of the data obtained from adolescents in York-town revealed four dimensions of identification which seemed conceptually meaningful. None of these dimensions directly involved traditional Judaism, although one item in the index dealt with a Christian holiday.

The dimensions of identification with which we will be concerned and the questions used to index them are as follows:

A. *Preference for Ethnic Group Companionship*

This dimension concerns the degree to which the adolescent limits his social associations to members of the ethnic group. It is assumed that teenagers who identify strongly with the ethnic group tend to choose companions from within the minority group.

1. "Do you ever date non-Jews?"

2. "Someday you may go to college and may want to join a fraternity (or sorority). Would you prefer to join one composed entirely of Jews or one composed of both Jews and Gentiles?" Respondents who stated they did not date non-Jews (54 per cent), or who preferred to join an all Jewish fraternity or sorority (26 per cent) were considered in-group oriented.

B. *Tendency to Emphasize Ethnic Group Solidarity*

This dimension concerns the extent to which the individual would encourage and promote group action that accentuated group distinctiveness and promoted group cohesiveness. We

believed that the adolescent who identified strongly with the
ethnic group would want to support programs designed to
preserve and strengthen the particularistic identity of the
ethnic group.

3. "At a conference I attended recently someone suggested
that the Jews in this country should celebrate a national
holiday of their own — something like the Irish celebrate
St. Patrick's Day. Perhaps the Jews could celebrate Israel's
independence day. How do you feel about this?" Respondents who favored this proposal (48 per cent) were
considered in-group oriented.

C. *Resistance to Adopting Out-group Practices*

This dimension deals with the individual's attitude toward accepting practices which might promote assimilation.
The in-group oriented adolescent tends to oppose the adoption of practices which blur religious differences or are
strongly associated with the out-group.

4. "Recently I read an article in which it was suggested
that it is alright for Jews to celebrate Christmas since it
is really a national holiday. I also know people who object
to this. With whom would you most agree?" Respondents
who opposed this suggestion (70 per cent) were considered in-group oriented.

D. *Opinion Orientation*

This dimension refers to the extent to which the individual
is affected by the assessments members of the ethnic group
make of him. The adolescent who identifies with the ethnic
group tends to be more oriented toward the opinion of
ethnic co-members than of persons outside the group.

5. "Whose opinion of you is most important to you —
the opinion of Jews or of non-Jews?" Respondents who
answered that the opinion of non-Jews was more important

to them than the opinion of Jews (34 per cent) were considered out-group oriented.

An analysis of the data revealed these questions to be positively inter-related. Hence, it was decided to sum each adolescent's responses to the five questions and to treat the result as a single identification score. As a means of simplifying the presentation of the data, the adolescents were divided into two roughly equal groups: those who gave in-group responses to three or more items (56 per cent of the sample) were considered relatively highly identified with their ethnic group; the residual category (44 per cent) were considered as being less identified with the ethnic group.

As Table 26 shows, the expected relationship between group identification and religious traditionalism did in fact exist. In attitude and overt behavior adolescents who scored relatively high on the identification index were significantly more likely to be traditionalistic than were their peers whose level of ethnic group identification was relatively low. Thus, we found that 40 per cent of the "high identifiers" held traditionalistic attitudes toward beliefs, 50 per cent were traditionalists in their orientation toward certain religious practices and 39 per cent were traditionalists in their actual behavior. In each of these areas the "low identifiers" were significantly less traditionalistic: 18 per cent accepted traditionalist beliefs, 23 per cent held traditional attitudes toward religious practices, while only 9 per cent followed traditional practices.

While these data were in line with our predictions, we were troubled by the fact that the small size of the sample made the introduction of a third variable into the table impracticable. A third variable in this analysis was clearly indicated, for we knew that religious traditionalism was highly correlated with the degree of traditional observance in the home. Perhaps what was actually being demonstrated in Table 26 was not so much

TABLE 26

*Relationship Between Adolescent's Level
of Ethnic Group Identification and His
Religious Attitudes and Behavior*

| | Level of Identification | |
	Low PER CENT	High PER CENT
Adolescent's Attitude Toward Beliefs		
Traditionalistic	18	40
Non-Traditionalistic	82	60
Adolescent's Attitude Toward Practices		
Traditionalistic	23	50
Non-Traditionalistic	77	50
Adolescent's Behavior		
Traditionalistic	9	39
Non-Traditionalistic	91	61
Total Cases§	22	28

§ These relationships are statistically significant at the .05 level or better as determined by the chi-square test using the Yates correction factor.

a relationship between identification and traditionalism as between traditionalism and the level of religious observance in the adolescent's home. Without controlling for the latter factor, it was impossible to be certain. However, when a third variable was introduced into the analysis of the Yorktown data, the frequency of cases in some cells became so small that statistical analysis was impossible.

Fortunately it was not necessary to leave the analysis in this unsatisfactory condition, for the Philadelphia and Nebraska questionnaires contained one of the items used in the York-town identification index: "It is alright for Jews to celebrate Christmas since it is really a national holiday?" While this item in itself is not an entirely satisfactory substitute for the Yorktown index, it has the advantage of bringing into use a larger sample and hence permitting a more extensive analysis of the relationship between identification and traditionalism. For this reason, the adolescent's answer to the "celebrating Christmas" question was treated as a rough index of identification and then cross-tabulated with his level of traditionalism in attitudes and behavior, while at the same time home environment was held constant.

As the data in Table 27 reveal, the relationship between identification and religious traditionalism persisted even when home environment was controlled. In both beliefs and practices, irrespective of whether he was from a traditionalistically oriented home or not, the adolescent who opposed the celebration of Christmas by Jews was significantly more likely to be traditionalistic than his peers who saw no objection to Jews celebrating Christmas.

The effect of identification upon religious traditionalism was most striking among adolescents from unobservant homes. In this group the high identifiers were five times as likely to be traditionalistic in beliefs, three times as likely to be traditionalistic in attitude toward practices, and nine times as likely to be traditionalistic in actual behavior than were low identifiers from a similar home environment. Even among adolescents from traditionalistic homes the high identifiers tended on the average to be twice as traditionalistic in attitudes and behavior as their relatively low identifying peers.

Group identification and the level of traditional observance in the home seemed to have a somewhat independent but cumulative effect on the adolescent's religiosity. Consider the two

TABLE 27

Relationship Between Attitude Towards Jews
Celebrating Christmas and Adolescent's Religious Attitudes
and Behavior with Home Environment Controlled

	Traditionalistic Home		Non-Traditionalistic Home	
	For Celebrating PER CENT	Against Celebrating PER CENT	For Celebrating PER CENT	Against Celebrating PER CENT
Adolescent's Attitude Towards Beliefs				
Traditionalistic	21	55	5	31
Non-Traditionalistic	79	45	95	69
Adolescent's Attitude Towards Practices				
Traditionalistic	31	66	7	24
Non-Traditionalistic	69	34	93	76
Adolescent's Behavior				
Traditionalistic	17	33	1	9
Non-Traditionalistic	83	67	99	91
Total Cases§	29	139	214	340

§ First Philadelphia and Nebraska samples only. Not including adolescents who left questions unanswered.

These relationships with exception of adolescent *behavior* among subjects from non-traditionalistic homes, are statistically significant at the .05 level or better as determined by a chi-square test.

polar types in Table 27: those teenagers who scored high on the identification index and whose home environments were relatively traditionalistic formed one group, and those adolescents who scored low on ethnic group identification and whose homes were relatively non-traditionalistic formed another. The first group can reasonably be considered as most receptive to traditional influences, while the second group should have been much less inclined towards traditionalism. This is in fact what the data very clearly show. The second group was the least traditionalistic of any group in the sample: only five per cent were traditionalistic in attitude toward beliefs, seven per cent in attitude toward practices and one per cent in their actual behavior. The first group, on the other hand, was the most traditionalistic of any cluster in the table: 55 per cent were traditionalistic in attitude toward beliefs, 66 per cent in attitude toward practices and 33 per cent in their behavior. Thus, both group identification and family environment can be said to contribute to the adolescent's religious convictions and conduct.

IDENTIFICATION AND GROUP SURVIVAL

Why is there, the reader may ask, a relationship between ethnic identification and adolescent religiosity? After all, there are other ways of showing one's attachment to the group. Early in this century, for example, a vigorous effort was made to strengthen the adolescent's ties to the ethnic group through increasing his interest in *secular* Jewish culture, while Zionism, before and since the birth of the state of Israel, has been a factor in promoting cohesion among some segments of the American Jewish community. How, then, does one explain the nexus between the two variables?

The answer, in part, seems to lie in the relationship many adolescents see between religion and group survival. Somewhat more than half of the Philadelphia-Nebraska samples, and an even larger proportion of the Yorktown group, 62 per cent, agreed with the statement,

> "If the Jews give up the observance of certain customs and rituals such as the dietary laws, circumcision, it would inevitably lead to the breaking up of Jewish life."

Also, 80 per cent of the Philadelphia respondents, and 66 per cent of the Nebraska group believed that "the Jewish people could not survive as a separate people without the synagogue."

Their concern over the group's survival appears to have been one reason why many adolescents, though non-traditionalistic themselves, were opposed to changes in the traditional code. Thus, we found that 36 per cent of the youngsters who reported eating non-*kosher* food "sometimes" or "often" were opposed to changes in the dietary code. This seemingly paradoxical finding prompted additional interviewing which uncovered two factors. First, many teenagers had a strong respect for orthodox Judaism and objected to changes which seem to them to violate its traditions. One 15-year-old girl, who did not observe *kashruth*, opposed any change in the dietary laws because,

> "That's the way its always been. I don't know; it just seems wrong to. After all, those laws were made long ago. What right have I to change them?"

Second, some non-traditionalistic adolescents felt that traditional ceremonial practices contributed to group survival and should be preserved for that reason. They believed that although the rituals were meaningless to them, they were "a good thing" for other people and for the group. This point of view was summed up by a 17-year-old boy:

> "Keeping *kosher* is a lot of ritual, like doing a lot of monkey dances. But I think they ought to keep it. It helps the Jews keep closer together."

Of course, the feeling that group survival is dependent upon the maintenance of certain religious rituals and institutions is not necessarily an indication of ethnic group identification: an individual may believe that religion is necessary to group survival and yet be indifferent to whether the group or its religion survives.

There is, however, a relationship between group identification and the belief that certain religious customs are essential to group survival. Adolescents in the Philadelphia-Nebraska samples were asked to respond to this statement:

> "If the Jews give up the observance of certain customs and rituals, such as the dietary laws, and circumcision, it will inevitably lead to the breaking up of Jewish life."

Fifty-one per cent of the adolescents agreed with this statement, 47 per cent disagreed and two per cent left the question unanswered. Using the "celebrating Christmas" item as an index of ethnic group identification, we can see in Table 28 that in-group-oriented adolescents were more likely to agree with this statement than were respondents who did not object to Jews celebrating Christmas: 66 per cent of the former felt that traditional religious practices were essential to group survival, as compared with only 29 per cent of the latter.

A belief that traditional religious customs are essential to ethnic group survival was found to be related, logically enough, to the adolescent's level of religious traditionalism. An inspection of the data in Table 29 reveals that a youngster who believed traditional customs to be essential to group survival was significantly more likely to be traditionalistic in attitude and overt behavior than one who did not assign to traditional practices this cohesive effect. Among the former group 36 per cent were traditionalists in attitude toward beliefs, 41 per cent in attitude toward practices and 16 per cent in overt behavior; among the latter, 15 per cent were traditional in their beliefs, 9

TABLE 28

Relationship Between Attitude Towards Jews Celebrating Christmas and Belief that Traditional Religious Customs are Essential to Jewish Survival

Are Religious Customs Essential to Jewish Survival?	Attitudes Towards Jews Celebrating Christmas	
	Favor PER CENT	*Oppose* PER CENT
YES	29	66
NO	71	34
Total Cases§	243	479

§ First Philadelphia and Nebraska samples only. Not including adolescents who left questions unanswered.

This relationship is statistically significant at the .01 level as determined by the chi-square test.

per cent in attitude toward practices and 5 per cent in actual behavior. While other factors no doubt contribute to this relationship it seems quite likely on the basis of these data that some adolescents are motivated to follow traditional customs out of a concern for the survival of their ethnic group.

GROUP IDENTIFICATION AND ASSIMILATION

Logically, the adolescent's level of identification with the ethnic group and his attitude toward assimilation ought to be closely related. But, in fact, no such relationship was found. The answer to this surprising discovery proved to be very simple: very few youngsters in this study favored the complete assimilation of the Jews into the general society. For example, when this prospect was put directly to Yorktown's teenagers in the form of the statement, "The Jews should give up their

TABLE 29

*Relationship Between Belief that Religious
Customs are Essential to Survival and the
Adolescent's Religious
Attitudes and Behavior*

	Are Religious Customs Essential to Jewish Survival?	
	Yes PER CENT	*No* PER CENT
Adolescent's Attitude Toward Beliefs		
Traditionalistic	36	15
Non-Traditionalistic	64	85
Adolescent's Attitude Toward Practices		
Traditionalistic	41	9
Non-Traditionalistic	59	91
Adolescent's Behavior		
Traditionalistic	16	5
Non-Traditionalistic	84	95
Total Cases§	386	359

§ First Philadelpha and Nebraska samples only. Not including adolescents who left questions unanswered. These relationships are statistically significant at the .05 level or better as determined by the chi-square test.

religion and become Gentiles," only 6 per cent of the group responded "agree". To the question "If you had a chance to be born again, would you rather be born a Jew or a non-Jew?" 76 per cent answered "Jew," 6 per cent "non-Jew," 18 per cent "don't know."

This preference for their ethnic identity was only in part a function of religious interest, however, as can be seen in the answers to the follow-up question "Why did you make this choice?" asked of adolescents who said they preferred rebirth as a Jew. Almost a third of the group (32 per cent) made reference to religion, of which the following comment was fairly typical:

> "I just like the Jewish religion. I don't like the ideas of some of the other religions, like marrying only once in the Catholic religion."

50 per cent preferred being Jewish seemingly more out of habit than conviction, as witness the following explanation:

> "I could say Gentile; it would be easier. But I've lived as a Jew; it's the only thing I know. I couldn't change."

The remaining 18 per cent could give no reason for their preference. The commitment to ethnic identity evident in these responses may reflect pride in group membership, habituation or possibly a reluctance to express sentiments which could be taken as an admission of inferiority. But it is also possible that our questions were taping a recognition on the part of adolescents in a small community that their ethnic identity was inescapable. Most adolescents in Yorktown felt that their ethnic group membership was known to all — 92 per cent of the youngsters said that everyone knew that they were Jewish. Hence, there was no escape. As one boy put it, "Everyone knows that I'm Jewish, so what's the sense of kidding myself."

Religion, then, is a significant factor in the adolescent's commitment to his identity; however, as was the case in our discussion of the meaning of ethnic identity and the identification of the adolescent with his ethnic group, the data show that other variables are at work. Nonetheless, it is clear that religion is a recurrent theme which permeates the thinking of many teenagers as they examine meaning of their identity and their relationship to the ethnic group.

Summing Up

The principal focus of this study has been on the group as a factor in the formation of religious attitudes and behavior among Jewish adolescents. Our strategy was first to examine the adolescent's response to a variety of traditional beliefs and practices and then to analyze the influence of four important groups (the family, the peer group, the minority group and the general society) upon his religious convictions and conduct. Thus, many aspects of the adolescent's religious viewpoint were presented, his behavior in a variety of situations reported and the pressures and influences which several groups exerted upon him within a small community analyzed. Wherever possible, the data were interpreted within the framework of reference group theory.

Out of the welter of percentages, statistical tables and analytical material in the previous chapters there emerged a picture, albeit fuzzy, of the adolescent's religious posture and of the role various groups played in its development. The purpose of this chapter is to describe, insofar as the data permit, the salient characteristics of this picture and to sum up the contribution some groups have made in the formation of adolescent religiosity.

ADOLESCENT RELIGIOUS ATTITUDES AND BEHAVIOR: AN OVERVIEW

The study began with an examination of the adolescent's position with respect to eleven traditional beliefs and practices. The position of the three major divisions in contemporary American Judaism were examined and the adolescent's own attitude or action reported. It would be useful to examine what appear to be the salient characteristics of the religious convictions and conduct of the teenagers in this study. We were able to discern four such characteristics.

Drift and Selectivity

The average adolescent in this study was neither a traditionalist nor a non-traditionalist. His exact position between these two extremes would be difficult to locate with any degree of precision, but it appeared closer to the non-traditionalist than to the traditionalist end of the continuum. Despite the fact that about three-quarters of adolescents were affiliated with Orthodox or Conservative congregations, only a small minority could be called traditionalists. Traditional attitudes toward a particular belief or practice were seldom held by more than half the sample, while often only a minority, sometimes less than 25 per cent of the adolescents, were traditionalists. More adolescents rejected a traditional belief or practice outright than accepted it.

On the whole, the adolescent tended to accept more traditional beliefs than practices, possibly because the observance of ceremonial rituals restricted his participation in the general society and circumscribed his behavior to a far greater extent than did the acceptance of traditional beliefs. A strict observance of the dietary code, for example, requires very precise, at times inconvenient and often conspicuous behavior. The belief in the Messiah or Chosen People concepts imposes far fewer restrictions on their action.

In some cases the adolescent's attitude or behavior represented a personal break with traditionalism, in others a perpetuation or enlargement of a break made by parents or grandparents. When the adolescent reported a change in attitude or behavior, it was more often away from traditionalism than toward it. Thus, it would seem that the drift away from traditionalism which observers reported a generation ago has not been halted. But it does not seem to be gaining speed and may in fact be slowing down. The predictions made a generation ago by worried prognosticators of a total abandonment of traditional Judaism by American youngsters have not been borne out.

Adolescents who turn away from the traditional beliefs and practices of their parents rarely abandon all aspects of their traditional training, perhaps because the contemporary adolescent, unlike many immigrant Jews of a generation or so ago, does not seem to feel that he must choose between accepting all of traditionalism or rejecting it outright. He tends to be highly selective. Very few teenagers were consistently traditionalist or non-traditionalist as regards all the beliefs and practices examined in this study. It was not at all uncommon for a youngster to accept one traditional belief and reject another, even though the position of his congregation was positive or negative towards both.

Discrepancy Between Attitudes and Behavior

Seemingly everywhere people find it easier to preach than to practice the traditional elements of their religion. The youngsters in this study were no exception to this rule. While considerable respect for the Orthodox viewpoint was shown by many adolescents, even by those who had not been reared in that tradition, their admiration was often merely lip service. Their behavior ofttimes seemed little influenced by their attitudes. Representative of this phenomenon were the adolescents who valued the Talmud as a repository of Jewish law and wisdom, but had never read any part of it. Some teenagers thought regular and frequent attendance at religious service admirable, but never attended services themselves.

The discrepancy between attitude and behavior was especially noticeable with respect to attendance at religious services and the observance of the dietary code. For example, although none of the adolescents attended religious services daily, four per cent favored such observance by others. Although only 17 per cent of the adolescents attended religious services once a week, 44 per cent felt that weekly attendance was highly desirable. The same pattern existed with respect to the dietary code: almost none of the adolescents thoroughly and consistently observed the food practices, yet 8 per cent felt that Jews should never eat non-*kosher* food at any time, while 33 per cent told us that non-*kosher* food might be eaten outside of, but never in the home.

If there is a strain towards consistency in attitude and behavior, as Murphy (1947) maintained, these inconsistencies should have created feelings of tension and guilt. Yet, we were able to discern little evidence of either from this source. Only infrequently did a teenager show marked signs of guilt when his behavior did not conform to the standards implicit in his attitudes. In many cases the teenager seemed either to have isolated attitudes from action so that he was unaware of the discrepancy between the two, or, as was more common, the discrepancy was rationalized away by pointing to similar inconsistencies among his peers. The following remark by a girl who did not observe the dietary code but felt that other people should is an example of a teenager justifying her behavior by pointing to similar violations by her peers. She described her first reaction to eating non-*kosher* food in this way:

> "You know when I first ate *tref* I almost got sick. Really I almost vomited I felt so bad. But now I've got so used to it I don't even notice it. You see, all the girls in my crowd do it."

Apparently when norms are commonly violated by one's peers, the guilt feelings which would ordinarily arise are not present or are quickly shrugged off.

Regional Similarities and Differences

Though separated by almost fifteen hundred miles in space and somewhat more than a decade in time, adolescents in the Eastern and Midwestern samples were far more like each other than they were different. With few exceptions the differences between Eastern and Midwestern teenagers in this study were not statistically significant. Interestingly enough, when Midwestern adolescents did differ from their peers in the East, it was the Midwesterner who tended to be the more traditionalistic of the two. This finding was surprising. We had expected Midwest teenagers to be less traditionalistic than Easterners, principally because the great centers of Jewish population and cultural influence are in the East.

The reasons for this unexpected finding are not clear. It may reflect the fact that the Midwestern sample was chosen from relatively small Jewish communities. Perhaps Jews in smaller communities, surrounded by a sea of non-Jews, tend to hold more tightly to traditional viewpoints: this was the case with Yorktown Jews when compared with their peers in Philadelphia. Or it is possible, though the evidence to support this conclusion is far from adequate, that during the decade between the first and last interviews, Jewish adolescents have moved somewhat in the direction of traditionalism.

Positive Orientation Toward Religion

Very few adolescents were militantly hostile to religion. Whatever form rebellion took among the Jewish teenagers in this study, it was seldom rejection of religion. Quite the contrary, most adolescents were favorably disposed towards religion. Many felt that religion was important and that it was desirable to be more religious themselves. Like their parents, the youngsters believed that religion was a "good thing" — a value which deserved general approval and support. But this broad positive orientation toward religion seemed to lack ego involvement. Religious subjects were discussed with a certain flatness of emotional tone and a distinct lack of fervour. Religious leaders found it difficult to arouse much excitement about religion among teenagers and even more difficult to get them to sacrifice time and energy to support religious activities.

Their generally friendly but non-enthusiastic approach to religion was in some ways more frustrating to religious leaders than outright hostility would have been, for at least the latter attitude indicates the presence of strong emotions. On the other hand, there was little opposition to programs merely because they had religious connotations, as was so common a generation ago, and the very lack of a hostile "set" toward religion could be one of the significant characteristics of the religious attitudes of Jewish adolescents today.

GROUP FACTORS IN ADOLESCENT RELIGIOSITY

Once the position of the adolescent on a number of religious issues was determined, we were able to turn our attention to the principal questions raised in this study. They were: To what extent does the position of the adolescent reflect the expectations and pressures of the various groups to which he belongs? Which of his many membership groups are important to him? Which ones specifically influenced him in religious matters? In order to answer these questions, our first task was to locate the adolescent's significant religious referents.

Location of Significant Referents

Two approaches were employed to find the adolescent's religious referents: First, we sought to determine which individuals or groups served as *models* for religious self-estimations. Second, the adolescent was asked whom he considered important to him, and more specifically which groups had influenced him so far as religion was concerned.

An examination of reference group theory and the data revealed that the referent may serve as a model or as a censor-opinion leader. In some cases, the same individual or group performed both functions, although this was not inevitably the case. Particularly interesting was the discovery that a large number of adolescents were using the Orthodox community and its norms as a model against which to evaluate their religiosity. The standards represented by this model were seldom observed in the behavior of individuals. The postulated or conceptual reference group served as an upper anchor for the adolescents' self estimations and was partly responsible for the generally moderate evaluations adolescents made of their religiosity.

A high proportion of the adolescents listed both family and peer groups as models and opinion leaders in religious matters. This was in agreement with our hypothesis that models were also likely to be opinion leaders in circumstances where the content of comparison was important to the individual. It will be remembered that more than 75 per cent of the adolescents said that religion was important to them. The general society or the ethnic community were seldom designated as religious referents. Yet their influence was believed to be so crucial that they were included among the four groups studied: the family, the peer group, the ethnic group, and the general society. Let us summarize our findings for each of these four groups.

The Family

This study attempted to supplement the parent-child correlation technique as a way of establishing a causal relationship between parent and child attitudes by *first* systematically determining whether in the adolescent's opinion parents were significant others, and *then* comparing the parents' expectations and behavior with the adolescent's attitudes and behavior.

After the adolescents' significant referents had been determined, we went on to examine the pressures these groups exerted upon the adolescents to insure the adoption of their norms.

Family pressures and expectations were the first to be examined. Adolescents in Yorktown were asked to evaluate parental religious expectations and the pressures put upon the teenager to see that these expectations were met. While parental pressures and expectations were found to vary somewhat from family to family, often reflecting idiosyncratic biases and religious affiliation, there appeared to be some expectations which characterized most adults in this study. An analysis of the adolescent's perception of adult expectations and conversations with adults indicated that most parents encouraged their children to adopt a positive attitude toward religion, to maintain some contact with other members of the group, and to observe a few religious practices, especially attendance at religious services.

A clear relationship was found between the adolescent's perception of parental expectations and his religious self-expectations, attitudes and behavior. Thus, youngsters who perceived their parents as having traditional expectations were far more likely to be traditionalists than their peers whose parents were perceived as not having such expectations.

The data also showed a positive relationship between parental behavior and adolescent religiosity; that is, the more traditionalistic the home environment, the more likely the adolescent would be a traditionalist in attitude and action. This was to be expected, given the family's strategic role in the socialization process. Still, it was reassuring to find that the frequent assumption that parents influence their children's religious attitudes and behavior was supported by systematically collected empirical data.

The Peer Group

The importance of the peer group for the development of religious attitudes and behavior among Jewish adolescents proved to be considerably greater than most adolescents — and their parents — believed possible. In Yorktown, where the adolescent was observed as he interacted with peers in various formal and informal settings, the peer group exerted a strong influence upon the adolescent. It was important, however, to distinguish between the influence of the formal and the informal youth groups. The formal youth groups were torn by clique rivalry, plagued by member apathy and devoid of a coherent religious program. Largely for these reasons their effect upon the religious attitudes and behavior of Yorktown's teenagers appeared to be minimal.

The informally organized clique moved into the vacuum left by the ineffectual formal youth groups. The clique's power over the teenager in Yorktown was remarkably strong partly because like most peer groups the clique gave him status and a sense of belonging at a time when conflicting loyalties, identifications and changing values made him unsure of himself. The clique's norms provided a frame of reference within which religious attitudes were formed and behavior channeled. These norms were enforced through various pressures exerted upon the adolescent to conform to the clique pattern. Some deviation from the norm was permitted, but beyond a point the deviant's behavior became unacceptable to the group. If he persisted in his error, he was penalized. In some instances teenagers were isolated from their peers because of a non-permissable violation of a clique norm.

The effect of peer group pressures upon the adolescent's religiosity could be seen in the high degree of similarity of religious convictions, conduct and self-evaluation among clique members. We found, also, that when the adolescent deviated from the parental religious pattern, he tended to conform to the peer group's norms. Sometimes the adolescent was caught between the cross-pressures of conflicting family and peer group expectations. When this occurred, and it did in a number of cases as regards the use of *kosher* food, it was the peer group which most often succeeded in determining the adolescent's behavior.

The Ethnic Group and the General Society

The adolescent's religiosity was examined in the context of his membership in two important secondary groups: the ethnic minority group and the general society. Each group put pressure upon the teenager to conform to its norms. In many areas the pressures were toward a common goal. But in the area of religion the pressures were sometimes opposed to each other, particularly if the adolescent was inclined to be a traditionalist.

The general society exerted pressures upon the Jewish adolescent which tended to alienate him from traditional Judaism by undermining his adherence to the religious beliefs and practices which stressed group separateness. These pressures were identified as the (1) pressure toward uniformity-conformity, (2) pressure toward secularization, and (3) pressure toward equalitarianism. They made it psychologically difficult for the Jewish adolescent to be different from the dominant majority, or to accept religious beliefs and practices which the general society regarded as queer or undemocratic.

Minority group pressures, for the most part, tended to strengthen the adolescent's ties with the ethnic group. In Yorktown these pressures were of two types — formal and informal. Examples of the informal pressure were the village ethos which characterized the Yorktown Jewish community and the actions of self-appointed guardians of the traditional code. These guardians, supported by the community's village-type climate of opinion, gave the Jew in Yorktown the feeling that he was being watched by the community and served as an effective agent of social control. By reinforcing the exogamy taboo, the village ethos helped channel the adolescent's social contacts within the ethnic group, and by continually reminding him that he was a Jew, it strengthened his sense of ethnic identity.

The Jewish Center and the religious school were examined as examples of formal organizations which might be expected to influence the adolescent's religious attitudes and behavior. We found that the Jewish Center in Yorktown was not particularly effective in this respect. As a secular organization, its influence upon the adolescent's religiosity was indirect and apparently negligible. The religious school was more energetic in this area, but only moderately more successful. An analysis of the data collected in Philadelphia revealed that information levels increased commensurate with increases in schooling, as did adherence to certain traditional religious beliefs and practices. The latter, however, was remarkably influenced by the degree of traditional observance in the home. The religious attitudes and behavior of adolescents from traditional homes were more likely to be affected by religious schooling than were their peers from non-traditional family environments.

Unless he is in some way isolated from their influence, the Jewish adolescent is pulled in opposite directions by the ethnic group and the general society, particularly in communities where the traditional system is supported by militant elements.

How he will resolve this conflict, which of the two groups he will favor will depend in part upon the degree of his identification with these groups. We believed that the more the individual identified with the ethnic group, the more likely it was that he would be a traditionalist in attitude and action. This, in fact, was what the data revealed. Using an index of identification consisting of questions unrelated to traditional Judaism, we were able to show that adolescents who identified strongly with the minority group were more tradition-oriented than those whose level of ethnic group identification was low.

This relationship between group identification and religious traditionalism seemed to be in part a function of the role many adolescents believed religion played in group survival. Adolescents who identified referentially with the ethnic group often stated that the abandonment of certain religious customs would inevitably lead to the breaking up of the group. The inference was that they were motivated toward religious traditionalism because of a desire to strengthen the group's chances for survival.

INFORMATION AND ITS USES: A CONCLUDING NOTE

One of the purposes of this study was to provide parents, professional workers and other persons interested in the religious life of Jewish adolescents with concrete information about the youngsters' religious convictions and conduct. How adults will respond to these data and to what use they will be put will depend largely upon their evaluation of its merit, and their own biases, values and goals. Traditionalists and religious educators may find the data disturbing, for the evidence is strong that some of the practices and beliefs of traditional Judaism had very limited appeal for many adolescents. Nor was religious education achieving the goals of informing and inspiring the Jewish student to the degree that educators hoped for. Non-traditionalists may be surprised to find that traditionalism as an ideal is still greatly respected by many adolescents and that traditional standards are still widely employed by adolescents of all religious complexions in evaluating the religiosity of themselves and others.

Whether traditionalists or non-traditionalists, many adults should find some aspects of these data reassuring, particularly those persons who have long feared that the Jewish community is "losing its youth" or that Jewish youngsters are becoming atheists. The data clearly indicated that most adolescents were opposed to assimilation and that in general they were oriented positively towards religion. Yet this positive orientation lacked enthusiasm and coexisted with marked confusion in the area of religious belief and practice. As we have shown, much of this confusion derived from the conflicts experienced by adolescents who belonged to an ethnic minority group in a highly secular heterogeneous society. The adult who wishes to help the adolescent must first know the nature of these conflicts and their sources — and then be prepared to guide the adolescent in his search for a religious system in which he can believe and with which he can live. For the Jewish youngster seems to be searching for guidance as to what to believe and how to behave, and a rationale for doing so with enthusiasm. There is, we believe, a latent reservoir of religious feeling among Jewish adolescents which has not yet been adequately tapped. The challenge and the opportunity which this study poses for parents and other adults interested in youth, traditionalists and non-traditionalists alike, is how to arouse and channel the latent enthusiasm and vigor that abound in Jewish adolescents. For, it is in the hands of youngsters such as those described in this book that the future of Judaism and the American Jewish community lie.

References

Abrahams, Israel, *Jewish Life in the Middle Ages*, New York: Macmillan, 1896.

Albo, Joseph, *Sefer Ha-Ikharin: Book of Principles*, Philadelphia: The Jewish Publication Society, 1898.

Allport, Gordon W., James M. Gillespie, and Jacqueline Young, "The Religion of the Post-War College Student," *Journal of Psychology*, 25, 1948, pp. 3–33.

Argyle, Michael, *Religious Behavior*, Glencoe: The Free Press, 1959.

Baron, Salo W., *The Jewish Community, Its History and Structure to the American Revolution*, Philadelphia: The Jewish Publication Society, 1942.

————, *A Social and Religious History of the Jews*, New York: Columbia University Press, 1952.

Bernard, Harold W., *Adolescent Development in American Culture*, New York: World Book Co., 1957.

Blos, Peter, *On Adolescence: A Psychological Interpretation*, Glencoe: The Free Press, 1962.

Child, Irving L., *Italian or American? The Second Generation in Conflict*, New Haven: Yale University Institute of Human Relations Publications, 1943.

Clark, Elmer T., *The Psychology of Religious Awakening*, New York: Macmillan, 1929.

————, *The Small Sects in America*, Nashville: Abingdon-Cokesbury, 1949.

Cloward, Richard A. and Lloyd E. Ohlin, *Delinquency and Opportunity: A Theory of Delinquent Gangs*, New York: The Free Press of Glencoe, 1960.

205

Cohen, Morris R. and Ernest Nagel, *An Introduction to Logic and Scientific Method*, New York: Harcourt, Brace, 1934.

Coleman, James S., *The Adolescent Society: The Social Life of the Teenager and its Impact on Education*, New York: The Free Press of Glencoe, 1961.

Davis, Kingsley, *Human Society*, New York: Macmillan, 1950.

Doob, Leonard W., "The Behavior of Attitudes," *Psychological Review*, 54, 1947, 135–156.

Elder, John, *Archaeology and the Bible*, London: Robert Hale, 1960.

Finkelstein, Louis, *The Beliefs and Practices of Judaism*, New York: Devin-Adair, 1945.

Franzblau, Abraham N., *Religious Beliefs and Character Among Jewish Adolescents*, New York: Harper, 1934.

Freud, Sigmund, *An Outline of Psychoanalysis*, New York: Norton, 1949.

Geismar, Ludwig L., "A Scale for the Measurement of Ethnic Identification," *Jewish Social Studies*, 1954, 16, 33–60.

Ginzberg, Eli, Sol W. Ginsburg, Sidney Axelrod, and John L. Herms, *Occupational Choice: An Approach to a General Theory*, New York: Columbia University Press, 1961.

Glazer, Nathan, *American Judaism*, Chicago: University of Chicago Press, 1957.

——— and D. P. Moynihan, *Beyond the Melting Pot: The Negroes, Puerto Ricans, Jews, Italians and Irish of New York City*, Cambridge: M.I.T. and Harvard University Press, 1963.

Glover, Alfred K., *Jewish Laws and Customs*, Wells, Minn.: W. A. Hammond, 1900.

Goode, William J., *World Revolution and Family Patterns*, New York: The Free Press of Glencoe, 1963.

Gordis, Robert, *Conservative Judaism, an American Philosophy*, New York: Harper, 1948.

Gordon, Albert I., *Jews in Suburbia*, Boston: Beacon Press, 1959.

Gordon, Calvin W., *The Social System of the High School: A Study in the Sociology of Adolescence*, Glencoe: The Free Press, 1957.

Gorer, Geoffrey, *The American People: A Study in National Character*, New York: Norton, 1948.

Gottlieb, David and Charles Ramsey, *The American Adolescent,* Homewood: The Dorsey Press, 1964.

Graetz, Heinrich, *History of the Jews,* Philadelphia: Jewish Publication Society, 1891.

Hall, Granville S., *Adolescence: Its Psychology and Its Relations to Psychology and Its Relations to Physiology, Anthropology, Sociology, Sex, Crime, Religion and Education,* New York: Appleton, 1905.

Hartley, Eugene L., May Rosenbaum, and Shepard Schwartz, "Children's Use of Ethnic Frames of Reference," *Journal of Psychology,* 1948, 26, 367–386.

Hirschberg, Grace and A. R. Gilliland, "Parent-Child Relationships in Attitudes," *Journal of Abnormal and Social Psychology,* 37, 1942, 125–130.

Hollingshead, August B., *Elmtown's Youth: The Impact of Social Classes on Adolescents,* New York: Wiley, 1949.

Hollingsworth, Leta A., *The Psychology of the Adolescent,* New York: Appleton, 1928.

Hyman, Herbert, "The Psychology of Status," *Archives of Psychology,* 269, 1942.

James, William, *The Varieties of Religious Experience,* London: Longmans, 1912.

Jersild, Arthur T., *The Psychology of the Adolescent,* New York: Macmillan, 1957.

Kaplan, Benjamin, *The Eternal Stranger: A Study of Jewish Life in the Small Community,* New York: Bookman Associates, 1957.

Kaufman, Yehezkel, "Anti-Semitic Stereotypes in Zionism," *Commentary,* March, 1949.

Kramer, Judith R. and Seymour Leventman, *Children of the Gilded Ghetto,* New Haven: Yale University Press, 1961.

Lazerwitz, Bernard, "Some Factors in Jewish Identification," *Jewish Social Studies,* 15, 1953, 3–24.

Lerner, Max, *America as a Civilization, Life and Thought in the United States Today,* New York: Simon and Schuster, 1957.

Linton, Ralph, *The Study of Man: An Introduction,* New York: Appleton-Century, 1936.

Lynd, Robert S. and Helen Lynd, *Middletown: A Study in Contemporary American Culture,* New York: Harcourt-Brace, 1929.

Mead, George H., *Mind, Self and Society,* Chicago: The University of Chicago Press, 1934.

Merton, Robert K., and Alice S. Kitt, "Contributions to the Theory of Reference Group Behavior," in *Studies in the Scope and Method of 'The American Soldier,'* " Robert K. Merton and Paul F. Lazarsfeld, (Editors), Glencoe: The Free Press, 1950, 40–105.

Merton, Robert K., *Social Theory and Social Research,* Glencoe: The Free Press, 1957.

Murphy, Gardner, *Personality: A Biosocial Approach to Origins and Structure,* New York: Harper, 1947.

Murray, Gilbert, *Five Stages of Greek Religion,* London: Watts, 1935.

Myrdal, Gunnar, *An American Dilemma: The Negro Problem and Modern Democracy,* New York: Harper, 1944.

Nathan, Marvin, *The Attitude of the Jewish Student in the Colleges and Universities Towards his Religion,* New York: Block, 1932.

Newcomb, Theodore M. and G. Svehla, "Intra-Family Relationships in Attitudes," *Sociometry,* 1, 1937, 180–205.

———, *Social Psychology,* New York: Dryden, 1950.

Orlinsky, Harry M., *Ancient Israel,* Ithaca: Cornell University Press, 1954.

Ortega y Gasset, Jose, *Revolt of the Masses,* New York: New American Library, 1950.

Philipson, David, *Old European Jewries,* Philadelphia: The Jewish Publication Society, 1894.

Radin, Max, *The Jews among the Greeks and Romans,* Philadelphia: The Jewish Publication Society, 1915.

Raisin, Jacob S., *The Haskalah Movement in Russia,* Philadelphia: The Jewish Publication Society, 1913.

Riesman, David, Nathan Glazer and Reuel Denney, *The Lonely Crowd: A Study of the Changing American Character,* New York: Doubleday, 1953.

Rose, Arnold and Caroline Rose, *America Divided,* New York: Knopf, 1948.

Rosen, Bernard C., "Multiple Group Membership: A Study of Parent-Peer Group Cross-Pressures, *American Sociological Review,* April, 1955, 155–161.

————, "The Reference Group Approach to the Parental Factor in Attitude and Behavior Formation," *Social Forces,* December, 1955, 137–144.

————, "The Achievement Syndrome: A Psychocultural Dimension of Social Stratification," *American Sociological Review,* April, 1956, 203–211.

————, "Minority Group in Transition," in *The Jews: Social Patterns of an American Group,* Marshall Sklare, (Editor), Glencoe: The Free Press, 1958.

————, "Race, Ethnicity and the Achievement Syndrome," *American Sociological Review,* February, 1959, 47–60.

———— and Roy D'Andrade, "The Psychosocial Origins of Achievement Motivation," *Sociometry,* September, 1959, 185–218.

————, "Family Structure and Achievement Motivation," *American Sociological Review,* October, 1961, 612–624.

————, "Family Structure and Value Transmission," *Merrill-Palmer Quarterly, January,* 1964, 59–76.

————, "The Achievement Syndrome and Economic Growth in Brazil," *Social Forces,* March, 1964 a, 341–354.

————, "Estrutura e Identisicacöes na Familia," *Sociologia,* June, 1964 b, 151–158.

Rosenau, William, *Jewish Ceremonial Institutions and Customs,* Baltimore: The Friedenwald Co., 1903.

Ross, Murray G., *Religious Beliefs of Youth,* New York: Association Press, 1950.

Rossman, Parker, "Religious Values at Harvard," *Religious Education,* 1960, 55, 24–30.

Samuel, Maurice, *Prince of the Ghetto,* New York: Knopf, 1948.

Shaw, Clifford R. *et al., Brothers in Crime,* Chicago: University of Chicago Press, 1938.

Sherif, Muzafer, "A Study of Some Social Factors in Perception," *Archives of Psychology,* 1935, 27, No. 187.

————, *An Outline of Social Psychology,* New York: Harper, 1948.

Shibutani, Tamotsu, *Society and Personality,* Englewood Cliffs: Prentice-Hall, 1961.

Sklare, Marshall, *Conservative Judaism, An American Religious Movement,* Glencoe: The Free Press, 1955.

———— and Marc Vosk, *The Riverton Study: How Jews Look at Themselves and Their Neighbors,* New York: American Jewish Committee, 1957.

———— (Editor), *The Jews: Social Patterns of an American Group,* Glencoe: The Free Press, 1958.

Smith, Ernest A., *American Youth Culture,* Glencoe: The Free Press, 1962.

Starbuck, Edwin D., *The Psychology of Religion,* London: Walter Scott, 1899.

Steinberg, Milton, *Basic Judaism,* New York: Harcourt, Brace, 1947.

Sullivan, Harry S., *Conceptions of Modern Psychiatry,* Washington: William A. White Psychiatric Foundation, 1947.

Stauffer, Samuel A., Louis Guttman, Edward A. Suchman, Paul F. Lazarsfeld, Shirley A. Star, and John A. Clausen, *Measurement and Prediction,* Princeton: Princeton University Press, 1949.

Thomas, William I. and Florian Znaniecki, *The Polish Peasant in Europe and America,* New York: Knopf, 1927.

Thrasher, Frederick M., *The Gang,* Chicago: The University of Chicago Press, 1927.

Whyte, William F., *Street Corner Society: The Social Structure of an Italian Slum,* Chicago: The University of Chicago Press, 1943.

Williams, Robin M., *American Society: A Sociological Interpretation,* New York: Knopf, 1960.

Wirth, Louis, *The Ghetto,* Chicago: The University of Chicago Press, 1928.

Zangwill, Israel, *Children of the Ghetto,* New York: Macmillan, 1919.

Index

211